What Can You Do with a Major in

EDUCATION?

What Can You Do with a Major in

EDUCATION?

Real people.

Real jobs.

Real rewards.

Jennifer A. Horowitz
and Bruce Walker

*Jennifer A. Horowitz,
Series Creator*

WILEY

Wiley Publishing, Inc.

WILEY

Table of Contents

Foreword

What can I do with a major in education?

Can you give me a list of jobs I can do if I major in education?

Should I major in X and minor in Y or major in Y and minor in X to be sure I'll get a great job?

How often I've heard these questions as a career counselor at a traditional liberal arts college. Concerns about "the major" are consuming to students from their first year through their last. At first it is the anxiety over choosing the "perfect" major; later it is concern that the major chosen may not have been the right decision.

Gone are the days when students felt they could major in anything they chose with no concern about their future careers. Managerial training programs that welcomed bright college graduates regardless of their academic backgrounds are rarely seen, and the world seems to get more and more specialized and require greater and greater focus and preparation from college graduates.

This series of books should ease much of the anxiety around the choice of major through its thoughtful exploration of possible career paths that lead directly from a specific major or which may at first glance seem completely unrelated. Much can be learned from the personal histories of individuals who majored in particular fields as well as from the rich resources in the Appendix.

Career development is a messy process. It can be seen as a dialogue between the self and the world. It involves interests, skills, values, and dreams. It requires an individual to be able to articulate her or his assets, whether they are transferable skills, abilities honed through jobs and internships, or passions fueled by community service—and whatever one has chosen for a solid academic foundation—one's major.

—Jane Celwyn
Director of the Office of Career Development
Barnard College, New York

About This Book

As young kids, we were allowed to experiment—play even—with different career ideas. Did you have a little medical kit when you were a child? Did you build architectural marvels with Legos? Did you style Barbie's hair *and* clothes so that she was ready for the red carpet? Did you use your chalkboard to teach the other neighborhood kids how to spell properly? Did you have fun playing at whatever career was your fancy that day, week, year, hour?

Even then, though, there was probably some pressure. The medical-kit parents were probably secretly thrilled and might have *casually* mentioned to neighbors and family members, "My daughter wants to be a doctor!" While parents might have worried about their safety, they also probably found common kid career choices such as firemen or policemen admirable. They probably liked the idea of little Vincent becoming an astronaut! But what about the child who wanted to drive a dump truck? Or the child who dreamt of being a bartender? Don't parents start to nudge (push even) children toward careers *they* find acceptable?

And the pressure doesn't stop there. The decision of "what are you going to do with life" escalates as you enter your last few years of high school. By the time you're ready to start college, you may be in an out-and-out panic about picking a major. And when you do decide on a major, the advice, judgment, criticism, and suggestions will be even more critical and intense. "You're majoring in philosophy? What kind of job can you get with a degree in philosophy?" Or "A psychology degree? Who hires people with a psychology degree in this day and age?"

As the economy has changed, college tuition and related costs have increased so dramatically that most students depend on varying degrees of student loans and financial aid, in addition to the sacrifices their families may make to send them to school. These expenses increase the pressure on students to choose a major based on its marketability, not just on their personal areas of interest. Students know that they may be stuck paying back loans for years after graduation, so they feel increasingly obligated to major in something that will lead to a job that can pay the bills. More pressure!

How This Book Helps You Make Smart Decisions

This book starts with this message: Relax! Sure some students know right away what they want to study and what they want to do, but the vast majority admit they don't know—or claim they do but secretly don't. That's okay. You should take your time and really think about what major is best for you, and that's the first main focus of this book.

Second, it's a myth that a major equals a career. Your major prepares you for a career, but not just one career. Your major provides you with lots of varied and different career options. That's the second major purpose of this book: To show you the variety of traditional and nontraditional careers you can pursue in education.

Third, the job market has changed and continues to change, and there's no magic major that will assure success. But you can learn how to make the most of your major and how to learn skills that are applicable and transferable to many different fields—making you more marketable. This book also focuses on helping you use your major toward a job that is financially and personally rewarding.

A Guide to This Book

The following sections describe some of the features you will find in this book. The book starts with a discussion of majors, colleges, additional education, and then careers, but you don't have to read the book from start to finish. Feel free to read the chapters in whatever order will be most helpful to you and your personal situation.

Chapter 1: Majoring in Education

If you have already decided on education or are leaning toward this major, read this chapter. You'll learn the basic requirements for this major, the types of courses you can expect to take, as well as general information and advice about this major.

Chapter 2: Choosing a College

If you are already in college, obviously you don't need help picking a college. If you haven't decided on a college, this chapter can help you determine the key factors to consider in general as well as in particular for education majors.

Chapter 3: Making the Most of Your Time at College

This chapter provides advice on how to make the most of your college career (beyond dating and parties!). Instead, you'll find that little things you can do throughout your college years can make a big impact later when you are about to enter "the real world."

Chapter 4: Attending Graduate School

Many majors, education included, require post-graduate studies. As you get into or look at an ideal career, you may consider getting your master's or terminal degree in education to make you more marketable and competitive. This chapter gives you the lowdown on graduate programs and ways to choose the best one for you.

Chapter 5: Career Possibilities for Education Majors

This is a key chapter of this book and describes both the traditional and non-traditional careers you can expect to get with a degree in education. The chapter gives a summary of the different types of careers, as well as salary and work environment information.

CHAPTER 6: BREAKING INTO THE JOB MARKET

This chapter contains some basic advice on transitioning from college life to the working world. It includes information on state certification, breaking into key education jobs, and solid advice on putting together materials that will make you marketable. In addition, you'll get some great advice on how to put your best foot forward in an interview.

CHAPTER 7: CASE STUDIES

In this chapter, you read about several people who graduated with an education major and who have used it to go into a variety of careers and achieve success. You'll be surprised at some of the jobs these people found as well as how the opportunities presented themselves. In these case studies, the participants describe their jobs and explain what they like and dislike about their work. They will tell you how they got to where they are today and discuss their successes and mistakes so that you can benefit from their experience.

RESOURCE APPENDIX

In the appendix, you will find a wealth of other information related to the education major and jobs, including

- ◆ Education organizations, with contact information
- ◆ Books ideal for education majors
- ◆ Magazines you might consider subscribing to

After reading this book, I hope you find many ways to make a living from a major in education—one that engages, challenges, and rewards you personally and financially!

Chapter 1

Majoring in Education

The United States Department of Education reports that education is one of the most frequently awarded college degrees in the nation. In recent time, close to 106,000 education majors have graduated from college each year. This may not seem surprising in a country with such a large population; the sheer number of children all but guarantees that the American education system is one of the nation's major employers, especially when day care, private and parochial schools, and other special programs are factored in along with the public schools. In fact, it is estimated that there are currently some 54,000,000 students enrolled in grades K-12, and approximately 3,400,000 teachers instructing them. What may be surprising is the number of liberal arts colleges and universities that do not offer education as an undergraduate major.

What sets the education major apart from other college majors such as English or mathematics is that it is connected to a professional field that is subject to state licensing and oversight. Although the requirements for a permanent teaching license vary from state to state, there are some commonalities, including the eventual completion of a master's degree in education. Some universities with graduate programs in education may choose not to offer an undergraduate major in the same field because many of the same courses constitute the master's program.

Still other colleges offer an education *minor* rather than a major, giving students the opportunity to explore the field a bit before deciding whether to commit to a graduate program. This also may give students an advantage when applying to graduate schools and when looking for jobs because their transcripts will reflect an early interest in education as well as in the subject they choose as their major. An education minor may actually involve more course work and credit than other minors because student teaching and other fieldwork add to the load.

A common theme in the literature provided by education programs of all sorts—major, minor, and graduate—is the almost sacred responsibility of teachers to the lives of other people's children and thus to the future of the nation. The nation's schools are charged with so many tasks, from integrating the children of immigrants to ensuring a competitive workforce, that teachers are forced to bring many different skills to their jobs. In addition to knowing the subjects they teach and the strategies for teaching children of a particular age, teachers are also called upon to teach everything from ethics and manners to hygiene and good nutrition. For this reason, education programs usually require interdisciplinary knowledge from a variety of related fields, as described in the following section.

Requirements

Most undergraduate education departments require students to begin with an *introductory course,* designed to provide an overview of the history and development of education in the United States, major theorists and their ideas, and the general methodology used.

Education courses are those offered directly by the college's education department and deal with educational issues, ranging from the very general to the very specific. General courses often have titles like "Foundations of Education," "The Culture of Teaching," or "Contemporary Issues in Education." More specific courses deal with curriculum development and techniques for teaching various subject areas and age groups (generally early childhood, elementary, and secondary or adolescent). Specialized courses concern the teaching of certain populations of students who differ from the mainstream, including minorities, the disabled, and those who do not yet speak English. Finally, colleges with a particular cultural or regional interest may offer courses on teaching related to that interest, such as teaching in religious or urban settings.

Related courses from outside the education program are courses offered by other departments but still critical for the development of a good educator:

- ◆ **Psychology courses** include developmental psychology or child development, the psychology of learning, and abnormal psychology. These courses provide an understanding of how students learn, enabling teachers to tailor their lessons to the type of students they will be working with. At colleges that offer an education minor rather than a major, students may choose to major in psychology to enhance their understanding of their students' mental processes.

- ◆ **Social science courses** include minority and ethnic studies, such as Latino, African American, Asian, and Native American studies. These courses provide an understanding of the many cultural and ethnic groups future teachers may encounter in their classes, particularly in large, multi-ethnic schools. In a related vein, many colleges require education students to take at least one course on cultural understanding and the avoidance of prejudice and discrimination. At colleges that offer an education minor rather than a major, students may opt to major in religious, ethnic, or women's studies so that they will be prepared to teach those populations.

- ◆ **Sociology courses** include courses on schools and classrooms as social environments, family dynamics and their role in student achievement, and the relationships between schools and communities. These courses provide an understanding of how schools are viewed by the many parties involved, including teachers, parents, political and community leaders, and students, and how these views affect the outcome of educational programs.

- ◆ **History courses** include the history of American education, patterns of migration and/or immigration in the United States, and specific eras of history, such as the Colonial period or the Cold War, as related to education. These courses provide an understanding of the role of education in American society, from the one-room schoolhouse to the "Americanization" of immigrants to the fight against Communism and the related focus on science education.

◆ **Health courses** include first aid, safety, and nutrition courses. These courses prepare teachers to assume responsibility for the physical safety and well-being of their students, especially in early childhood and elementary school settings, where teachers must supervise playtime, lunchtime, and snack time in addition to lessons.

◆ **Economics courses** include courses related to financing the educational system, from large city districts to individual classrooms. These courses provide an understanding of how economic policies affect school reform, technology, and teacher salaries, as well as such controversial issues as school choice and testing.

◆ **Philosophy courses** include courses on classical thinkers, such as Socrates and Plato, and on entire schools of thought and how they view the relationship between teachers, students, and society. These courses provide an understanding of how the role of education has been viewed throughout history.

◆ **Political science courses** include courses on various political and economic systems and the role of education in each. These courses provide an understanding of how education has been used to indoctrinate citizens and prepare them to fill needed positions in society.

◆ **Courses on subjects that may be taught in schools** are on those subjects that a teacher may specialize in teaching, such as English, math, history, the sciences, and foreign languages, among others. Students planning to teach in elementary schools may have to take a variety of these subjects, as many subjects are taught in one elementary classroom. Those who plan to teach at the secondary level may pursue more advanced courses in just one of these disciplines. In fact, those colleges that offer an education minor in lieu of the major may require the student to major in the subject(s) that he or she plans to teach.

◆ **Student teaching and fieldwork** provide academic credit for supervised, hands-on experience. Student teaching is required for state certification, and involves several hours a week assisting an experienced teacher in an appropriate classroom setting. The student teacher may work with small groups of children, prepare and teach certain lessons, and learn from the actions of the supervising (or cooperating) teacher. An accompanying weekly seminar or meeting with an advising professor in the education department allows the student teacher to discuss these experiences, ask questions about them, and put them into context.

Other fieldwork may include classroom observations with specific goals. In some cases, the goal may be to observe how a particular subject is taught. In other cases, it may be to follow a certain program or technique being tried in a classroom. Still other observations may involve following a particular student, especially one with special needs or who represents a certain demographic. Again, a related seminar allows students to share their observations and report on them.

Statistics on Education Degrees*					
	Associate's Degrees (2-year colleges)	Bachelor's Degrees (4-year colleges)	Master's Degrees	Doctoral Degrees	All Degrees
Public Colleges and Universities	7,853	75,786	72,719	4,785	161,143
Private Colleges and Universities	1,366	29,780	56,347	1,931	89,424
All Colleges and Universities	9,219	105,566	129,066	6,716	250,567

* National Center for Educational Statistics, 2002

Typical Requirements for Education Majors

Requirement	Purpose of Requirement	When the Requirement Is Fulfilled	Typical Choices
Introductory course	To provide an overview of the field; a prerequisite for all other education courses	Freshman or sophomore year	Foundations of education, exploring education, the culture of teaching, contemporary issues in education, introduction to early childhood/primary/secondary education, introduction to special education
Education department courses	To develop relevant skills and knowledge of disciplines in education	Throughout the college years	*Skills:* Curriculum development, observation and assessment of students, measurement and evaluation, classroom management and discipline, special education, deaf education, education of the gifted *Disciplines:* Literacy, the teaching of elementary school reading and language arts, the teaching of elementary school math, the teaching of elementary school science, the teaching of elementary school social studies, the teaching of secondary school English, the teaching of secondary school math, physical education, the teaching of secondary school biology/chemistry/physics/computers, the teaching of secondary school history, the teaching of secondary school foreign languages, the teaching of English as a second language, art education, music education

Related courses from other departments	To develop interdisciplinary knowledge and an understanding of other issues affecting education	Throughout the college years	Developmental psychology, child psychology, human learning and memory, abnormal psychology
			Urban studies, Latino studies, African American studies, Asian studies, women's studies
			Discrimination in American culture, cultural sensitivity, prejudice in the workplace
			Family dynamics, the culture of the schoolhouse, community development and growth
			History of American education, immigration and assimilation in the United States, the Cold War and American culture, the Industrial Revolution
			Child safety, nutrition, urban health
			School finance, state and city budgets
			The Socratic method, Western thought, the ideal of the Greek citizen, Eastern philosophies
			Totalitarian societies, the individual and the socialist system, capitalism and socioeconomic struggle

continued

Typical Requirements for Education Majors (continued)

Requirement	Purpose of Requirement	When the Requirement Is Fulfilled	Typical Choices
Courses on subjects to be taught	To develop expertise in a particular discipline	Throughout the college years	*English:* Medieval literature, the American novel, poetry, Shakespeare *Math:* Calculus, non-Euclidean geometry *Science:* Biology, chemistry, computer science, physics *History:* Ancient civilizations, the Renaissance, European history, Colonial America, World War II, the Cold War *Foreign languages:* French, Italian, Japanese, Spanish, Russian, and so on: beginning through advanced levels, the literature of, and so on
Student teaching, fieldwork, and practica	To gain hands-on experience and observations	Junior or senior year	Supervised student teaching, observation of the Montessori method, senior practicum in elementary education
Not-for-credit workshops and training	To develop preparedness for emergency situations	Junior or senior year	Child abuse awareness, cardio-pulmonary resucitation, first aid, fire department safety, and evacuation training

Finally, in light of the increasing awareness of child abuse and neg-lect, teachers-in-training are now required by many states to participate in workshops or seminars on recognizing and reporting such incidents. These sessions may be brief and thus may not accrue any academic credits, but because they are required for certification, many college education programs offer them on campus.

Skills Required to Succeed with the Education Major

For many years, education was considered a good profession for women because it required skills that were considered to be natural female char-acteristics, including patience and a nurturing instinct. Although this kind of thinking is now largely dismissed as stereotyping, the fact remains that there are certain skills and traits—regardless of gender—that are helpful for education majors to have, even for those people who go on to less conventional jobs.

- ◆ **Organizational skills** are helpful for any college student, but particularly for education majors, who must not only keep track of their own assignments, but also of the work they assign to numerous pupils in their student teaching placements. The abil-ity to stay organized is a big advantage in juggling all the respon-sibilities, people, and tasks involved in education.

- ◆ **Detail orientation** is an invaluable skill for similar reasons. Education majors are taught to design curricula, teach and assess students, and record all kinds of information, and having a good eye for detail makes it easier to keep up with all these tasks.

- ◆ **Public speaking skills** help education majors communicate effectively. These skills include speaking at the right volume so that everyone can hear, enunciating clearly so that the words are understood, and using appropriate vocabulary for the audience. Education majors are often judged on speaking ability because the trait is so important in the classroom.

- ◆ **Non-verbal communication skills,** which include writing, are important for similar reasons to public speaking skills. Not only will these skills help education majors with their own assignments, but they will also help on the job, when it will be necessary to give clear directions and present information clearly.

◆ **Flexibility** is needed to help education majors cope with unexpected changes. Student teachers must often adapt to schedule changes, shortages of materials, and children who need extra help. These situations can't be predicted, so it's useful to be able to find an alternative way of meeting goals on the spur of the moment.

◆ **Patience** is another important trait during unexpected situations. In addition to coming up with flexible solutions, it's crucial for a teacher to remain calm and maintain control of the situation. Failing to do so might discourage students or even cause a panic.

Challenges with the Education Major

The education major involves a lot of fieldwork outside of the college. In addition to attending classes, completing assignments, and studying, education majors must find time to fulfill student-teaching requirements—equivalent to working at a part-time job during the school year. Moreover, student teaching also involves "homework" in the form of planning lessons, grading assignments, and meeting with supervising teachers and professors. Students considering the education major must be prepared to make these commitments.

Another consideration about majoring in education is that it incorporates many government regulations that students must fulfill. Because education majors will be working with children, at least in a student-teaching capacity, they are subject to local laws intended to protect children. These laws differ by city and state, but they usually require fingerprinting and a background check, a seminar on child abuse awareness, and a clean bill of health. This last requirement may include testing for specific medical conditions and immunizing against certain diseases. Furthermore, education majors must pay fees to the appropriate government agencies and medical professionals for these services—an expense that doesn't come up for students in other majors!

The Perception of Education Majors

Teaching as a career has undergone some major image changes over the years. One hundred years ago, it was considered a suitable occupation for unmarried women who wanted to earn some money. It was an acceptable job for these women in terms of both their safety—they could go home while it was still daylight—and their reputation, because they would be surrounded by innocent children rather than men. However, it was understood that once a teacher got married, she would give up her job.

Decades later, when more and more women began working outside the home, teaching remained an acceptable choice. The school day ended early, enabling married teachers to go home on time to get their husband's dinner on the table and tend to their own children. In addition, working with children was seen as something women were naturally equipped to do, so to a large extent, women entering the teaching field were steered toward elementary schools. Male teachers were more likely to be employed by high schools, especially in traditionally "male" subjects such as math and science.

As time went by, however, world events led to an increased focus on education as a skilled profession. One oft-cited milestone was *Sputnik,* the Soviet spacecraft that took the United States by surprise and raised concerns that American education was lagging behind, especially in the sciences. No longer was it a matter of teaching basic skills and acclimating immigrants' children to American life. Now there was a big push to prepare students for the new demands of an increasingly competitive world. This led to more research into how children learn and how best to teach them. Soon there was increased focus on attracting, training, and retaining the best teachers possible. Today, this can be demonstrated by increased licensing requirements, including master's degrees, and by attractive benefit and retirement packages, even when base salaries are limited by budget constraints.

These events and trends have also influenced education in non-school settings. When *Sputnik* raised concerns about America's competitive edge, the effects went far beyond the schools. Corporate training also received a lot of attention. Instead of simply having a more experienced employee "show the ropes" to coworkers, companies began to put a lot of effort into developing training manuals and videos, retreats, on-site classrooms, and staffs of training specialists. Other businesses arose that specialized in teaching professional skills for workers to take back to their companies. These skills may involve computer literacy, operating equipment, team building, sensitivity training, and numerous other areas of relevant knowledge.

With the increased interest in education, both inside and outside the schools, there has been a corresponding increase in education-related support services in other businesses, from the publishers that provide textbooks and training manuals to the television networks that produce educational programming. Toy manufacturers want their games to teach social, mental, and motor skills. Product packaging designers and public service agencies want their literature to teach the public about health, nutrition, and safety concerns. Companies like these have all discovered the advantages of hiring education professionals to achieve these goals.

Chapter 2

Choosing a College

In this chapter, you'll find information that will help identify the criteria you'll use to select the school that's right for you, including

◆ Identifying financial criteria for selecting a school

◆ Identifying personal criteria for selecting a school

◆ Transferring from one school to another

◆ Understanding the current education field

◆ What to look for in a college

◆ Tips for applying to a school

Logistical Criteria

When selecting a college, the most important (and obvious) factors to consider are the ones that may seem the most mundane. These are also the issues that present the most immediate concerns, because in many instances you have no control over them. Among the factors to explore other than whether the school possesses a solid education program, are

◆ Tuition expense and financial aid

◆ Cost-of-living expenses in the college's geographical location

◆ The distance from your hometown

TUITION EXPENSE AND FINANCIAL AID

Benjamin Franklin declared that the only two things in life that are certain are death and taxes. If Franklin had lived in recent times, he might have added: "increases in college tuition."

It's a fact: A college education is an expensive proposition for most students and their families. Determining whether a college is affordable or not, however, isn't always easy. If you're a high school senior considering colleges and money is a major factor in your decision, don't automatically assume that a school is out of your price range. Many universities offer financial aid packages and scholarships that can make even the priciest education affordable to some students, particularly those who can prove financial need, have maintained a high grade point average, and have tested well on college entrance exams.

Other financial options also exist, including student loans. The government subsidizes several programs for students who display financial need, including

◆ **Federal Direct Loans.** If the college you select participates in the program, Federal Direct Loans are sponsored by the Department of Education, which provides the college with federal monies that the college loans to you at the same rates offered through private banks and credit unions. Federal Direct Loans offer a wide variety of repayment options.

◆ **Federal Perkins Loans.** If your college participates in the program, it may be worth your while to check out Perkins; students may be eligible to borrow up to $6,000 per year for a maximum of $40,000 (including Perkins loans taken out for graduate school). A Perkins loan offers a low interest rate of 5 percent, which does not accrue unless you are attending school less than half time. Repayment of the Perkins begins nine months after you graduate or fail to qualify as a half-time student. In addition, you have ten years to repay the loan.

◆ **Federal Stafford Loans.** Stafford loans are obtained through your bank, savings and loan, or credit union. A subsidized Stafford loan requires the government to pay your loan's interest while you attend school. With an unsubsidized Stafford loan, you are responsible for paying the interest, but you pay only the interest—and none of the principle—while you are in school. Applicants for a Stafford loan may qualify for a maximum of $138,500 combined for undergraduate and graduate degrees. Interest rates change from year to year, and are capped at 8.25.

COST-OF-LIVING EXPENSES IN THE COLLEGE'S GEOGRAPHICAL LOCATION

Most incoming freshman are required to live on-campus, which, believe it or not, can be a financial relief if you attend a school in a location known for its high cost of living, such as New York City, San Francisco, or Chicago. In fact, dormitories make good economic sense in that, for one relatively modest fixed fee, you can get a room, utilities, and meals.

The dorm life and married housing isn't for everyone. You should, however, be aware of how expensive off-campus housing is, especially if you are a returning student or a transfer student, or if you foresee yourself moving out of the dorms after your freshman or sophomore year. Before renting an apartment or house, it's always a good idea to ask for receipts for past utility bills to give you and your potential roommates an idea of how much money you'll need to budget for electricity and gas. The last position a college student wants to find him or herself in is deciding whether to buy propane to fill a heating fuel tank or purchase books for the semester.

Other factors to consider include whether you'll need a vehicle while in college, or whether you can rely on public transportation, walking, or bicycling. Will you have to pay a fee to the university for the privilege of owning a car? Will you have to pay extra for parking privileges?

THE DISTANCE FROM YOUR HOMETOWN

At first glance, this may not seem like an important issue—but once you've been stranded during a holiday break in your college town with no other living being in sight because everyone's gone home, you definitely will reconsider! Some incoming freshmen are prone to homesickness during their first semesters in college, and a quick weekend visit home can be just the cure—if for nothing more than to see family members and friends, and enjoy a home-cooked meal, or to persuade Mom to do your laundry!

Consider how easy it will be for you to return home for the holidays, summer break, or family emergencies. If a return trip home requires a plane trip, you'll want to make sure you have an emergency fund in the bank to purchase a last-minute plane ticket.

Identifying Personal Criteria for Selecting a School

Whether you're about to enter college for the first time, are returning to college, or are transferring from a different school, you need to assess the criteria that are most personal to you when you select a college to attend.

◆ What are your long-term goals and what schools would best fulfill them?

◆ Where do you wish to live after graduation?

◆ What schools offer the best education for an academic major/minor?

◆ What is the school's reputation?

WHAT ARE YOUR LONG-TERM GOALS AND WHAT SCHOOLS WOULD BEST FULFILL THEM?

If you're just beginning college after high school, some of these questions may seem a little complex. After all, sometimes it's hard to determine whether you even possess long-term goals when you're 17 years old. It's highly recommended, however, that you give these questions considerable thought before selecting your college. If you find that you cannot come to any definite conclusions on your own, sit down with your parent(s), guidance counselor, or favorite teacher(s). One or all of these people may have insights into your character that might not be apparent to you.

Determining your long-term goals before selecting a college may save you a lot of time—and expense. Selecting a college that does not meet your educational requirements may require you to transfer to another college in the future—and the new college may not accept all of your credits.

WHERE DO YOU WISH TO LIVE AFTER GRADUATION?

Once you've established your long-term goals, you may have some idea as to where you'd like to live and work after you graduate from college. Obviously, if you want to live in a rural setting, it doesn't make a lot of sense for you to attend a university that focuses primarily on urban education programs. Believe it or not, there are distinct differences.

Of course, answering this question honestly before you've graduated from high school could be difficult. If you grew up in a city and don't know anything else, you may not know if you'd like to work anyplace else. The same is true if you grew up in a suburban or rural area. If you haven't experienced city life, you may not know whether or not it'll agree with you. But if you know you'd like to work in either the inner city or in the country, you should tailor your college selection accordingly.

WHAT SCHOOLS OFFER THE BEST EDUCATION FOR AN ACADEMIC MAJOR/MINOR?

High school guidance counselors should have access to information about which schools have the best reputations for education curricula, as well as good reputations in the subject(s) in which you'll specialize. If they do not, do some homework. Some publications, such as *U.S. News & World Report,* publish an annual ranking of U.S. colleges in such graduate programs as education, business, and engineering. Rest assured, if the school is ranked highly for its graduate programs, then its corresponding undergraduate programs must excel as well.

You likely will find it easy to determine which subject you want to focus on for your minor. Basically, think through the subjects you've enjoyed or excelled at in school—those that you think would be fun to teach others. If you're unsure about how to choose which subjects to major and minor in, talk with an academic advisor, who may be able to help you sift through your academic interests in order to determine what subjects you would be best able to teach. Advisors and counselors may also assist you by administering a survey questionnaire of your interests.

A quick inventory of your interests might include such questions as:

◆ What subject did my favorite instructor teach?

◆ What is my natural talent in the subject I am considering majoring/minoring in?

◆ What subjects hold my interest enough that I would consider a long-term career as an instructor in those subjects?

◆ What subjects are most in demand for new teachers?

WHAT IS THE SCHOOL'S REPUTATION?

The school you select will have two reputations—one for academics and another for socializing. Socializing can mean anything from an active sports program where invigorated students and alumni regularly congregate to show their school spirit to the reputation most college administrators dread: a party school.

The school's academic reputation should be your primary focus, but it would be unrealistic to believe that a university's social reputation wasn't a factor in most students' decisions on where to attend college. For many students, college is the first time they've been away from home, and college life offers them a chance to learn and apply interpersonal and socialization skills. However, some students ruin a school's reputation by freely interpreting "socialization skills" as rampant partying and binge drinking.

Transferring from One School to Another

College is a period of personal growth. You'll learn a lot about yourself in a highly charged educational atmosphere. One thing you may learn is that the college you initially selected does not fit your needs any longer. Perhaps your original criteria have changed. Or circumstances require you to move to another geographical location. Or perhaps you're returning to college after previously dropping out. Each of these situations will require you to transfer to another university.

If your circumstances allow it, you can take advantage of your previous college experience to find a school that fulfills all of your educational, social, financial, and geographical requirements rather than simply selecting the nearest one that will accept you. Perhaps the most important question confronting you as a potential transfer student is how many of your credits from your previous school will transfer to your new college.

Although it may be economically expedient for you to attend the college that accepts the majority or all of your previous credits, you may be doing yourself a disservice. In some instances, universities offer a highly integrated curriculum of coursework. These curricula provide the most value to the students who take them from start to finish, rather than in the piecemeal fashion of a transfer student who joins in midstream.

Take the time to research your prospective university's curriculum. If you cannot determine for yourself, you may need to set up an appointment with the department chair. He or she may arrange for you to speak with a faculty advisor who can help you decide whether you're prepared to join the educational program in progress, or if your educational needs will be best served by starting from the beginning.

Understanding the Current Education Field

The entire education playing field has been changed dramatically by recent government programs that insist on teacher and school system accountability. The national No Child Left Behind Act and various state programs have required school systems to make significant alterations in education methodology. If you intend to major in education and work in the public school system, you need to be convinced that the school you select will prepare you for the current shifts in education philosophy and government involvement.

The federal No Child Left Behind Act requires not only that teachers earn a bachelor's degree and be fully state certified, but that they also possess a high level of competency in the subject area being taught. For grade school teachers, this means you must pass a test on your competency in math, writing, and reading. The Act also specifies that grade school certification—which formerly qualified you to teach from kindergarten through middle school (either eighth or ninth grade)—specifically applies only for kindergarten through sixth grade. Middle and high school teachers may also have to pass a test on the subject they are expected to instruct, if they are not already degreed in that specific subject area.

Making the Decision: Important Questions to Ask

Now that you've established your personal criteria, it's time to look at what different colleges offer. With the numerous college choices available to you, there are several important questions you should ask of a prospective university. When you talk to the college recruiter, be sure to ask the following questions:

◆ Who does the actual teaching of courses: professors or teacher assistants? Larger universities generally rely on teacher assistants—students who are working on graduate degrees—to teach undergraduate courses. While many teacher assistants may be perfectly fine instructors, many also lack the years of experience of an established professor with a doctorate degree. You need to find out how much supervision is available from the faculty for students who have never taught a class before?

◆ What is the academic environment of the university's education department? Some colleges subscribe to the "publish or perish" paradigm. This means that professors are promoted, granted tenure, and paid according to how many books and articles they publish. Published faculty is a great way for a university to market itself as a haven for extremely bright intellectuals. But a potential downside could be that professors are more engaged with furthering their own careers by researching and publishing their pet projects rather than providing you with the benefit of their experience, research, and knowledge.

◆ What percentage of the school's education majors/minors pass state certification? This information should be readily available from the school or in some of the resources listed in the appendix. Having this knowledge should give you an indication of how well a particular school will prepare you to pass state certification and licensure tests.

◆ Does the school offer interesting extracurricular/social activities geared toward education majors? For example, SUNY Albany hosts the Future Educators' Club, which is a pre-professional club for graduate and undergraduate students interested in exploring career options in the field of education.

◆ Does the college under consideration work hard to place its graduates? Where do the college's graduates end up teaching?

◆ If you're not sure that you want to teach, does the school offer alternative instruction that prepares you for an education job outside of teaching?

◆ If you already have a bachelor's degree in an area other than education, is it necessary to start an education program from scratch, or can you complete a post-baccalaureate program or a master's in education?

◆ Is the college geared more toward undergraduate programs in education, or more research-oriented for master's and doctoral students?

Another big consideration in selecting your college is the school's student-teaching program. For example, some schools offer traditional semester-long student-teaching programs during your senior year.

Others, however, require you to finish your bachelor's degree before beginning a student-teaching assignment, and then require you to fulfill a yearlong internship—unpaid internships for which you continue to pay tuition. This latter program has advantages: These programs are often highly regarded, which could mean better job offers or graduate school placement following graduation. But they also add another year of expense and schooling to a typical four-year program. You need to carefully investigate the student-teaching program of any school you're considering attending to be sure it fits into your and your family's budget and timeline.

Chapter 3

Making the Most of Your Time at College

Choosing a major is only one piece of the puzzle when you're looking at how to make the most of your college years. This chapter focuses on how to maximize your opportunities as a student so that you leave college with a rich experience, and you're best equipped to get into the career or graduate program of your choice. Of course there'll be opportunities to enjoy newfound freedoms—especially if you're on campus and away from home—and we don't want to minimize those opportunities. But keep in mind that financial assistance and landing a great job or graduate program placement after college are often based on your performance in your freshman and sophomore years, so you don't want to neglect your academic achievements. It's best to hunker down and take your classes seriously to ensure your future success.

Selecting Majors and Minors

Undergraduate education students typically minor in a specified subject matter. Graduate students typically get their master's in education, although there is a preponderance of those in the education field who feel it is to their advantage to earn their master's in both education and a specialized subject area.

You likely will have an idea of the subject you'd like to minor in. Maybe you have a knack for history or a great love of science. You'll likely identify these interests when you're still in high school—when a particular subject ignited your imagination, or a particularly charismatic teacher captured your attention long enough to inspire your interest in the subject the instructor taught.

More and more, colleges and universities require students to take prerequisite courses in a wide variety of subjects during the freshman and sophomore years. This would include subjects in the humanities, sciences, and mathematics. The rationale behind these courses is to introduce you to subjects to which you might never have been exposed, and, of course, to broaden your overall knowledge. If your college has such a program, these courses might be an opportunity for you to recognize an aptitude or high interest in a subject for which you had previously never given a second thought.

If you know you want to major in education but haven't chosen a subject in which to concentrate, consult with an academic or guidance counselor. Counselors often can help you determine which direction to take simply by discussing your likes and dislikes, grades in particular subjects, research papers you've previously written, and your academic predispositions to either liberal arts or science classes, as well as to elementary or secondary school students.

If you choose to enter an elementary education program, a minor isn't considered necessary in most cases, as most grade school teachers are expected to provide a general overview of such core subjects as mathematics, science, and reading comprehension. Choosing a minor, however, may make you more marketable to prospective employers—particularly if your minor is in a foreign language.

If you're still stumped about an area of concentration, your guidance counselor can assist you with tests to help you and your counselor gauge your personality type and interest levels in a wide variety of subjects and career options.

Giving Yourself a Competitive Edge

More and more, college education departments are encouraging students to exhibit a history of working with children prior to applying for an education major or minor. This may include volunteer work done while still in high school, but may also include work done prior to signing your major (typically before your junior year). Not only does this experience help you determine whether you'll enjoy working with young people in the future, it also gives you a competitive edge after graduation. Potential employers will be impressed that you view working with young people as more than a paycheck. Whether or not your college requires it, more experience is never a downside, and sometimes can prepare you nearly as much as education classes. Below are some experiences you might explore to strengthen your marketability:

- ◆ **Tutor.** Seek out a local school and offer your assistance as a tutor in your subject area of interest.

- ◆ **Teacher assistant.** Some schools allow college students to assist teachers with curriculum planning, teaching, and homework grading. This is a great opportunity to get your feet wet in education.

- ◆ **Sunday school teacher.** Because these positions seldom pay, many church education programs are understaffed. You can gain tremendous experience by tapping this resource.

- ◆ **Assistant sports coaching.** Grade school, high school, travel teams, and intramural teams are great ways to gain experience working with young people.

- ◆ **Assistant coach and judge.** Secondary school forensics and debate teams typically are screaming for assistants and one-on-one coaching for competitors, and competitive events are often woefully short of qualified judges.

- ◆ **Boys and girls groups.** Research what groups exist in your area, and look for a way to apply your knowledge and skill set to their—and your—advantage.

- ◆ **Student government advisors.** Middle school and high school student councils are a good way to introduce a prospective government teacher to practical applications of theories.

- ◆ **Office assistant.** If your goal isn't to teach, it would be beneficial to gain administrative experience by assisting in the office of a principal, superintendent, or guidance counselor.

Joining the Club

One of the most important resources available to any professional individual is a network of people with similar interests and career goals. The same holds true for education majors. You can meet like-minded students just like you by joining honor societies such as Kappa Delta Pi or campus-based organizations.

KAPPA DELTA PI

Kappa Delta Pi is the International Honor Society in Education. The society is dedicated to supporting professional growth for educational professionals at more than 550 campuses worldwide. Kappa Delta Pi sponsors workshops and conferences, publishes books and journals, offers scholarships and grants, promotes community service projects, and maintains a teacher hotline, employment resources, and professional development services.

Your college may not have a Kappa Delta Pi chapter, but you can still join online at www.kdp.org. The society requires that undergraduates be at least second-semester sophomores, have a minimum of 12 credits of education courses completed, and have earned a 3.0 out of a 4.0 grade point average. Graduate students must have 12 credits of education courses—six hours from an accredited institution—and at least a 3.25 grade point average.

FORMING YOUR OWN CLUB OR STUDY GROUP

Some schools have campus-based clubs that can give you a leg up in the education field—for example, the Future Educators' Club of SUNY at Albany. Such clubs offer you opportunities to seek career mentors, network, and trade experiences and information with other students. Look for such clubs at your college, or, if none exist, discuss with your academic counselor the possibility of starting one.

If all else fails, organize or join a study group of like-minded individuals. Here are some activities you might want to try:

◆ Have each member subscribe to an education journal, or assign each member a journal to which the college's library already subscribes, for articles to copy and discuss.

◆ Compare lecture notes and handouts from classes that are similar in nature but taught by different instructors—if one professor's perspective and methods are good, two or three are even better.

◆ Scan recent books on education theory and pedagogy for discussion and/or debate. Education is a political hot potato and there's no shortage of books that fall on either side of the ideological divide.

◆ Become politically active. Like it or not, politics and education are inextricably linked, and if you'll be in the education field, you should educate yourself on issues of school budgets, government and public calls for accountability, assessment testing, vouchers, charter schools, and state and national union activity.

◆ Volunteer as research assistants for professors who are writing papers and analyses of current and historical issues in education.

◆ Initiate an Education Issues column in the school's student and alumni publications. Students can work together or individually on a series of topical articles related to trends in education that might be of interest to the publication's readership.

◆ Organize or attend seminars and workshops for fellow classmates; spreading the wealth of the combined knowledge of your group to those outside the group will assist you in your organizational and presentational teaching skills.

Internships

Internships are a great way for students to gain valuable learning and career skills. An internship can either be a part-time or full-time position for a company or group where you will ideally learn aspects of the business that are closely aligned with your major. Full-time internships usually are summer positions, and part-time internships either are offered during the summer months or arranged to accommodate your other classes.

Most internships that are arranged through your college are for college credit. However, you may arrange an internship on your own for no college credit if you think it might help you with your career plans. Additionally, most internships offer little or no pay. Before you begin an internship without pay, you may wish to negotiate a stipend—a cash reward—that at least covers the cost of the credit hours you'll receive.

Internships are rare for individuals seeking an education degree, as most students who are preparing for teaching certification spend a semester student teaching. While many students perform internships during or between their junior and senior years, education majors seeking a career in teaching seldom have available credit hours for an internship. However, for students looking for a career in education that doesn't require teaching in a classroom, there may be opportunities to intern with companies that prepare lectures, education materials, and seminars for corporate clients and adult education classes.

If you determine that an internship will help you with your future career and educational goals, the first person you'll want to visit is your college guidance counselor. He or she will have a list of potential companies with which to intern. If you have no luck there, another good source for internships are nonprofit agencies in your community. Many nonprofits can't afford to pay interns and volunteers, so they therefore use a lot of free help—which you can use for work experience and college credit.

If you still can't find an internship, use a little ingenuity. Contact businesses in your area to determine whether they hire interns, and market yourself as if you were applying for a full-time job. Have a resume handy that lists all relevant work experience and skills that the company might be able to use. Make certain that the company wanting to hire you is interested in helping you develop the experiences and skills you'll need to market yourself after graduation. Believe it or not, some unscrupulous employers view interns as nothing more than cheap labor. Some of the businesses you may want to approach for an internship are listed below:

◆ **Computer training companies.** Rapid advancements in technology, programming, and software upgrades have kept computer training schools busy, which means that training materials continuously must be revised and edited, and employees continuously retrained—both good experiences for someone seeking a degree in education and good job experience.

◆ **Creativity seminar companies.** Several national training schools provide on-site training designed to unlock participants' latent creativity, and exercise booklets need to be written and edited, and trainers need to be hired.

◆ **Education publishing companies.** The increased focus on the importance of education has led parents to seek outside assistance in the form of workbooks for their children. In addition, the rise of home schooling has increased the need for affordable curriculum materials.

◆ **Nonprofit groups.** United Way agencies, American Red Cross, and other nonprofits often have community education programs that require educational materials and trainers.

◆ **Local businesses.** Insurance and investment companies are only two industries that regularly seek to educate current and potential clientele with newsletters and training seminars.

◆ **Library education programs.** Public libraries often offer educational programs in literature, film, history, and the arts. An intern can help prepare materials, set up course materials, market education events, and serve as a presenter.

Students seeking an internship in a related field should work closely with their school's guidance counselor for a placement that is most beneficial. However, a student who displays a little initiative may land him or herself a plum internship.

Student Teaching

Student teaching typically occurs some time in the fourth or fifth year of an education major or minor. The prospect often sounds daunting to students, but rest assured that you can prepare yourself before stepping in front of a classroom.

It is a good idea to meet with your assigned school and teacher well in advance of the scheduled semester. This will give you an opportunity to assist the appreciative teacher, as well as learn what topics you will be teaching. Familiarize yourself with the books that will be used for the classroom. This exercise will be a great asset in your self-confidence when you finally get the opportunity to teach. While you are reading the materials, be sure to underline words and concepts that are unfamiliar so that you are not embarrassed or caught off guard when the reading comes up in the classroom.

When you meet with the teacher, go over his or her lesson plan, and ask specifically where you will be filling in. A good mentoring teacher will have established dates for the lesson plans for which you will be responsible. Familiarize yourself with the workbooks and assignments that will be used for your lessons. Try to establish time each week when you can meet one-on-one with your mentoring teacher to discuss your progress and seek suggestions for improving your skills.

Make yourself available to assist in other ways, including grading papers, tutoring, creating bulletin boards, and observing classes of other teachers in the school.

In addition, teachers recommend that their student teachers make their presence and availability known. Stopping by the school office to offer assistance raises your visibility and creates positive feedback among the faculty and administration.

Write a letter to your students and their parents to introduce yourself. The letter should give a brief educational background, outline what you will be teaching, and detail your availability to students and parents.

Remember that availability is important. You will make a very poor impression if you consistently seem to be in a hurry to make engagements outside the school. Your mentoring teacher may not look kindly on you if it appears your social life or outside commitments are interfering with your dedication to the classroom.

Mentoring teachers are used to dealing with novice teachers like you. Therefore, most of them are patient and willing to work with you to help you achieve your goals and derive as much from your student-teaching experience as you can. But any time two strangers meet, there's a chance that they will not get along. If this happens to you, remember that your time working with a difficult mentoring teacher is finite—in a few month's time, you'll be back in school or seeking a job. Keep your complaints to yourself or, at the very least, to a minimum. Provoking a confrontation with your mentoring teacher may cause a negative backlash that could impact your chance of finding a job later.

Even more difficult for some student teachers is the experience of a difficult classroom. Your textbooks and professors may have given you tips to deal with unruly students, but student teaching is really where the rubber meets the road. Work closely with your mentoring teacher to devise methods that will improve classroom discipline.

Even the best preparation available sometimes falls short, and you may find yourself dealing with a difficult classroom for an entire semester. The simplest advice here is to do your best and go the distance. Bring as many resources to bear on the problem as you can; it'll be a valuable learning experience for you to take into your career. Some of the resources may include your mentoring teacher, the school principal, or your professors.

Despite your best efforts, you may discover that teaching is not really for you. Work with your college advisor to help tailor the remainder of your academic career to an education career that does not require teaching children and adolescents.

As your student-teaching tenure comes to an end, be sure to express your appreciation to your cooperating teacher and school principal. Write thank-you cards to all faculty and administration members who have given you assistance during your student-teaching semester.

Some Financial Advice

Many education majors cite graduating with a huge debt as a major reason for abandoning a career in education for more financially but less emotionally satisfying employment. Although students may feel that an education career is their true vocation, they leave the profession because they couldn't wait long enough to receive tenures and pay increases. It is estimated that at least one-third of all education graduates leave their preferred careers—an attrition rate that could be reduced significantly with sensible financial planning.

Education graduates seldom earn outstanding salaries immediately after college (mid-$20,000 to $30,000 is the normal range). For this reason, you need to make every effort to live within your means while working toward certification so that you can avoid cumbersome, unnecessary debts upon entering the "real world." True, you might need to take on student loans in order to get your degree, but you don't need to take on a huge Visa bill outfitting your dorm room with a PlayStation 2 system and a surround-sound stereo.

The same goes for recent graduates who may or may not be paying off student loans. If possible, recent graduates should immediately begin saving money for ongoing education needs so that further education (whether a post-baccalaureate or master's degree) won't mean further debt. It's true that it's difficult to save money when earning only $25,000 a year, but every financial analyst will tell you that savings are an important part of fiscal responsibility—even if it's only $30 a paycheck.

The two most troubling debts students and recent graduates accrue are credit card debts and automobile payments. If possible, avoid credit card debt in any way you can. Remember that credit cards aren't free money; they're borrowing against your future, often at crippling interest rates. Before you put anything on your credit card, ask yourself whether you really need to make the purchase. If you have no other means for buying schoolbooks, the answer might be yes. If you're about to purchase a new pair of boots that everyone on campus is wearing, however, the answer is going to be no.

Also, beware of buying a new car; these often carry very high interest rates for students and also mean high insurance payments. As an alternative you may look into public transportation, carpooling, or purchasing a reliable used vehicle. Used cars often can be purchased outright, eliminating the need for bothersome monthly payments, or for substantially lower monthly payments.

Finally, look at your housing budget. While you're a student, make every attempt to economize on housing costs—without sacrificing personal and property safety and physical health—by foregoing expensive apartments or dwellings that are conveniently located to social activities and popular hangouts. Remember that every dollar you don't spend in college may result in enormous savings after graduation, because you are saving yourself from piling up debt that you'll have to repay someday.

Chapter 4

Attending Graduate School

T his chapter explores some of the topics pertaining to graduate school, including the following:

◆ What to look for when selecting a school

◆ When to apply

◆ Admissions tests

◆ Accreditation

◆ Methods of paying for graduate school

◆ Top U.S. graduate schools

If you receive your undergraduate degree and are planning to teach, chances are you'll end up in graduate school at some point. Most, if not all, states require teachers to attend graduate school in order to receive continued certification. Teachers must immediately complete at least 21 hours of study, and continue to add course hours every few years throughout their careers. Most get master's degrees in either education or their specific subject area. Those who want to specialize get degrees in special education, social work, reading, curriculum, or professional development.

Deciding what graduate school to attend usually depends on your employment situation. If you are already a certified teacher, chances are you'll want to attend a graduate program nearby. If you are entering graduate school immediately after receiving your bachelor's degree, or if you're returning to school in order to switch careers, you have a bit more freedom to select from the hundreds of accredited master's and doctoral programs available in the United States.

What to Look for When Selecting a School

You'll be investing a lot of money and hard work at the school you eventually attend. Before you select your school, make sure the school is prepared to work equally hard for you. Research the tough questions based on your bottom line, such as the school's record for job placement and the accomplishments of the school's previous graduate students.

Other areas to explore are the size of the school, the quality of the teaching staff, affordability, location, financial aid packages, and admission requirements. What types of programs does the school offer to ensure you get the most out of your post-graduate career? Does the school have a good library? What about computer facilities?

If possible, discuss the school with recent graduates in order to find out their experiences. Did they feel the school adequately prepared them for their careers?

Because we live in the information age, it's easy to find out about almost any graduate institution via the Web. Visit your prospective school's Web site. Using the information you find there, contact the department head for an interview.

Applying to the School

When should you apply? ASAP—as soon as possible. If you're considering attending graduate school, you should apply at least one year before you begin your graduate degree. Most applications require you to write a short piece on what you hope to accomplish as a graduate student. Be short and to the point. Include your important accomplishments, but don't try to cram your entire autobiography into your application.

You can assume that the graduate school to which you apply will ask you to submit references or recommendations. Professors usually are good sources for references or letters of recommendations, but other good references might include the principal and mentoring teacher at the school where you performed your student teaching. If you are a returning student, talk with your employer, coworkers, church clergy, or leaders in any professional associations you're involved in to get letters of recommendation.

Taking Admissions Tests

Graduate students usually are required to take the Graduate Record Examinations (GRE). You should plan to take the GRE a year or so before you apply for graduate school. Test results are available within two weeks if you take the computer-based GRE, and six weeks if you take the paper-based GRE.

The GRE consists of the General Test and eight subject-specific tests in Biochemistry, Biology, Chemistry, Computer Science, Literature, Mathematics, Physics, and Psychology. Don't worry; you won't be tested in each of the subjects! You'll only be tested in the subjects that most closely match your undergraduate major or minor. You will be given 2 hours and 50 minutes to complete each of the subject tests.

The General Test covers verbal and quantitative reasoning and writing skills. The General Test is broken into a 30-minute verbal component, a 45-minute quantitative component, and a 75-minute writing component. Depending on the college administering the test, a research and/or another verbal or quantitative component might be added. These components vary in length, and typically are not added to your final GRE score.

You can read more about the GRE at www.gre.org. You can also order a copy of the GRE Information and Registration Bulletin from:

Graduate Record Examinations
Educational Testing Service
Princeton, NJ 08541-6000
Phone: 609-771-7670

Accreditation

Most graduate schools require that you have an undergraduate degree from an accredited university. Accrediting agencies are governed by the U.S. Department of Education and the Council for Higher Education Accreditation (CHEA). Most of these agencies are regional, and the accreditation should be listed on the school's Web site and in the school's recruitment materials. Contact these agencies directly with your questions about the school in question.

For information on education accreditation, contact:

National Council for Accreditation of Teacher Education
2010 Massachusetts Avenue, NW, Suite 500
Washington, D.C. 20036
Phone: 202-466-7946
Email: ncate@ncate.org
Web site: http://www.ncate.org

Teacher Education Accreditation Council (TEAC)
One DuPont Circle, NW, Suite 320
Washington D.C. 20036
Phone: 202-466-7236
Email: teac@teac.org
Web site: http://www.teac.org

Financial Help You Don't Need to Pay Back

Many education graduate students are already certified teachers, and therefore gainfully employed. But low starting salaries and other concerns may require you to obtain some form of financial aid.

The broad range of financial assistance for graduate students in education makes it well worth your time to research. In the end, you may uncover a means by which you can pay for a portion if not all of your education. This section walks you through some of those options.

FELLOWSHIPS, GRANTS, AND SCHOLARSHIPS

Fellowships, grants, and scholarships are, as the song says, money for nothing. That is, it's money you don't need to repay, but awarding them is usually a hit-or-miss proposition as there are usually thousands of applicants, making the process very competitive.

Fellowships and scholarships in education usually are given to students who have earned high grades. You can apply for fellowships before you enter a graduate program, as well as while you're enrolled in the program. You should explore the fellowship programs available at the Council of Graduate Schools' Web site at http://www.cgsnet.org/ResourcesForStudents/fellowships.htm.

Grants are awarded based on financial need or a proven knack in education. If you're lucky enough to win a grant, there's a good possibility that not only your tuition, books, student fees, and supplies will be paid for, but also a portion if not all of your living expenses, including the living expenses of your dependents.

ASSISTANTSHIPS

When selecting your graduate program, check the availability of assistantships, which are a common way for graduate students in education to receive financial aid. Ideally, the university should offer assistantships that are specific to your area of speciality.

If you earn a teaching assistantship, there's a good possibility that you will receive a salary and your tuition will be reduced or totally reimbursed. As a teaching assistant, you will usually teach classes in your area of study or grade papers for professors.

As a research assistant you may work with a professor or department member to research a particular subject within your area of specialty. One positive aspect of a research assistantship is the opportunity for you to research your own papers, theses, and dissertations.

If you're willing to dig a little deeper in search of the elusive dollars to pay for your graduate degree, you may want to look into an assistantship at a residence hall, which may include free room and board, tuition, and salary. A counseling assistantship (rare but possible in education) might require you to advise undergraduate students or perform office work.

FEDERAL WORK STUDY

Federal monies are available at some universities to assist you should you want to work at a nonprofit public or private agency. Be forewarned: You will have to prove financial need for Federal Work Study. If you do qualify, 75 percent of your salary will come from the government, and the remaining 25 percent will come from the nonprofit.

LOANS

If you don't qualify or aren't successful in obtaining fellowships, grants, scholarships, assistantships, or Federal Work Study, don't be disheartened. Many different opportunities for loans are out there. Of course, you have to repay the loans, but often repayment is at rates significantly below the rates of commercial loans.

DEFERRING UNDERGRADUATE STUDENT LOANS

Already paying back a student loan for your undergraduate degree? Don't worry; Federal Stafford Loans and Federal Perkins Loans (see the next section) can be deferred—which means that you don't have to repay them as long as you are enrolled in school. This option comes in handy when budgeting for graduate school, as you'll have one less payment to make every month.

Don't just assume that your lending institution will know that you have enrolled in graduate school, however, and will automatically grant you a deferment. Contact your bank or credit union to let them know your situation. They will send you the necessary forms to fill out before you miss a payment.

FEDERAL LOANS

The government sponsors several different loan programs for college students based on financial need. Federal Direct Loans, Federal Stafford Loans, and Federal Perkins Loans are three options available to you. All federal student loan programs require you to fill out a Free Application for Federal Student Aid (FAFSA). Your parents don't have to co-sign the loan, and you don't need perfect credit to get a loan; the loans are determined by financial need rather than your credit rating. The FAFSA is administered by the U.S. Department of Education. The application can be downloaded at http://www.fafsa.ed.gov. You may either apply online or submit the application to the address on the form.

Federal Direct Loans. You can apply for a Federal Direct loan directly through your school—if your school participates in the program. If it does, the program works like this: The Department of Education provides the college with federal monies that the college loans to the student at the same rates offered through private banks and credit unions. The Federal Direct loans have a distinct advantage over the Perkins and Stafford programs because the Direct program offers a wider variety of repayment options. These options can be a real help if you foresee financial difficulties upon graduation.

Federal Perkins Loans. You also apply for Federal Perkins loans through your college—if your college participates in the program. Some colleges only offer Perkins loans to undergraduate students. But it may be worth your while to check out Perkins; graduate students may be eligible to borrow up to $6,000 per year for a maximum of $40,000 (including Perkins loans taken out as an undergraduate). The Perkins offers a low interest rate of 5 percent, which does not accrue unless you are attending school less than half time.

Repayment of a Perkins loan begins nine months after you graduate or fail to qualify as a half-time student. In addition, you have 10 years to repay the loan.

Federal Stafford Loans. You apply for a Stafford loan through your bank, savings and loan, or credit union. A subsidized Stafford loan requires the government to pay your loan's interest while you attend school. With an unsubsidized Stafford loan, you are responsible for paying the interest, but you pay only the interest—and none of the principle—while you are in school.

Graduate students applying for a Stafford loan may qualify for as much as $18,500 per year, up to a maximum of $138,500 combined for undergraduate and graduate degrees. Sound good? There is a downside: Interest rates change from year to year, and are capped at 8.25. (The 2002–03 rate is 4.06 percent.)

SUPPLEMENTAL LOANS

Private institutions may offer loans for graduate school that do not rely on federal funds. Such loans require a credit report, so if you've defaulted on a loan or had a car repossessed, chances are you won't qualify. But if your credit record is in pristine shape, or if you have a wealthy uncle or parent willing to co-sign, you may be in business. Another downside of privately funded loans is interest rates; because the loans are not federally guaranteed, banks, savings and loans, and credit unions may charge much higher interest rates than federal loans would charge.

Some private loan lenders and their respective Web sites appear below.

CitiAssist Loans. Citibank Corporation offers graduate students loans intended to supplement other financial aid packages. Check out the Web site at www.studentloan.com.

EXCEL Loan. If you already know that you can't qualify for a loan on your own due to poor credit or no credit at all, you may apply for an EXCEL loan with a co-signer who has a clean credit record. For more information, go to www.nelliemae.com.

Graduate Access Loan. The Access Group offers graduate student loans provided you maintain a half-time status at school. For more information, go to www.accessgroup.com.

Signature Student Loan. The government program Sallie Mae offers graduate student loans. For more information, go to www.salliemae.com.

Top Graduate Schools

Each year, the magazine *U.S. News & World Report* publishes a rundown on the best graduate schools in a variety of categories, including education. The schools are ranked according to scores in such categories as follows:

◆ Peer assessment (5.0 highest)

◆ Superintendent assessment (5.0 highest)

◆ Mean GRE scores verbal/quantitative

◆ Ph.D. and Ed.D. acceptance rate

◆ Student/faculty ratio

◆ Degrees granted

◆ Percentage of Ph.D. and Ed.D. students

◆ Research monies

As you might imagine, Harvard University and Stanford University consistently rank at or near the top of the annual list. Other universities that consistently rank high are UCLA, Vanderbilt University, University of Wisconsin-Madison, and Michigan State University. This section explains a bit more about the programs at each of these top-rated schools.

HARVARD

Teacher preparation: Master's degree in education with internship and preparation for licensure

Specialized programs: Education administration and supervision; education policy; educational psychology; higher education administration; curriculum and instruction, secondary teacher education

Peer assessment: 4.3

Superintendent assessment: 4.8

Entrance requirements: Includes GRE General Test or MAT, TOEFL, or TWE

Acceptance rate for master's degree programs: 65 percent

Acceptance rate for doctoral degree programs: 14 percent

Web site: http://www.gse.harvard.edu

STANFORD UNIVERSITY

Teacher preparation: Master's degree in education with internship and preparation for licensure

Specialized programs: Education administration and supervision; education policy; educational psychology; higher education administration; curriculum and instruction, secondary teacher education

Peer assessment: 4.6

Superintendent assessment: 4.7

Entrance requirements: Includes GRE General Test

Acceptance rate for master's degree programs: 54 percent

Acceptance rate for doctoral degree programs: 9 percent

Web site: http://ed.stanford.edu/suse/index.html

UCLA

Teacher preparation: Master's degree in education with internship and preparation for licensure

Specialized programs: Education administration and supervision; education policy; educational psychology; higher education administration; special education; elementary teacher education; student counseling; curriculum and instruction, secondary teacher education

Peer assessment: 4.0

Superintendent assessment: 4.6

Entrance requirements: Includes GRE General Test

Acceptance rate for master's degree programs: 54 percent

Acceptance rate for doctoral degree programs: 9 percent

Web site: http://www.gseis.ucla.edu

VANDERBILT UNIVERSITY

Teacher preparation: Master's degree in education with internship and preparation for licensure; alternative post-graduate program for provisional licensure

Specialized programs: Education administration and supervision; education policy; educational psychology; higher education administration; curriculum and instruction, secondary teacher education

Peer assessment: 4.1

Superintendent assessment: 4.6

Entrance requirements: Includes GRE General Test

Acceptance rate for master's degree programs: 68 percent

Acceptance rate for doctoral degree programs: 15 percent

Web site: http://peabody.vanderbilt.edu

UNIVERSITY OF WISCONSIN–MADISON

Teacher preparation: Master's degree in education with internship and preparation for licensure

Specialized programs: Education administration and supervision; education policy; educational psychology; higher education administration; curriculum and instruction, secondary teacher education

Peer assessment: 4.4

Superintendent assessment: 4.2

Entrance requirements: Includes GRE General Test

Acceptance rate for master's degree programs: 42 percent

Acceptance rate for doctoral degree programs: 34 percent

Web site: http://www.wisc.edu/grad

MICHIGAN STATE UNIVERSITY

Teacher preparation: Five-year baccalaureate program

Specialized programs: Education administration and supervision; education policy; educational psychology; higher education administration; curriculum and instruction, secondary teacher education

Peer assessment: 4.2

Superintendent assessment: 4.2

Entrance requirements: Includes GRE General Test

Acceptance rate for master's degree programs: 55 percent

Acceptance rate for doctoral degree programs: 46 percent

Web site: http://www.educ.msu.ed

Chapter 5

Career Possibilities for Education Majors

Salaries in education vary widely depending on the type of institution. Public schools depend on government funding and are affected by state and local budget and population. Private schools depend on tuition fees and donations and often have wealthy benefactors. Religious schools are classified separately here because they cannot be presumed to serve a wealthy population. Some religions have their own education "departments" that supervise and fund schools, much like the public schools, while others are independent and rely on tuition and donations, which depend on the socioeconomic setting of the population served.

Careers Teaching in K-12 Settings

These careers almost always require a teacher's license from the state, although exceptions may be made in certain settings, such as religious institutions. State licensing requirements vary so much from state to state and from one year to the next that it can be difficult to keep up, but most are considered provisional until the teacher earns a master's degree, which must be completed within a certain amount of time, taking into account that the teacher is working full time and can only go to graduate school in the evening and over the summer. In recent years, many of the states have begun to cooperate on license reciprocity, meaning that a valid teaching license from one state will be accepted in other states, much like a driver's license would be.

States and localities may vary in how they classify different grade levels. For example, in some places, kindergarten is grouped with nursery school as part of preschool or early childhood, while in others, kindergarten is part of the elementary school system. Similarly, grades 1–12 may be broken into elementary and high school (1–8 and 9–12); elementary, middle, and high school (1–5, 6–8, and 9–12); or elementary, junior, and senior high school (1–6, 7–9, and 9–12). As a result, some states are forced to offer different or overlapping licenses, and some aspiring teachers may find themselves having to get more than one license from the same state!

DAY CARE TEACHER

You provide a safe, nurturing environment for babies and young children whose parents are at work or school during the day. You prepare and conduct age-appropriate activities; encourage socialization, language development, and other skills; and provide physical care, such as feeding infants, providing meals for toddlers, and changing diapers. In addition to providing child-care, you are also concerned with preparing the children for success in school when they get older. The mean annual salary for day care teachers is $31,000.

PRESCHOOL TEACHER

You prepare lessons and teach children between 3 and 5 years of age. Because these children are so young, you must help them with many non-academic skills and tasks, from tying their shoelaces to proper hand washing. You need a great deal of patience and discipline for this job. Other responsibilities include conferring with and advising parents and evaluating children for age-appropriate development, skills, and socialization. The mean annual salary for preschool teachers is $32,000.

ELEMENTARY SCHOOL TEACHER

You prepare lessons and teach children between first grade and the end of elementary school. You are responsible for teaching a wide variety of academic subjects, so you must have a broad base of knowledge and good organizational skills. Other responsibilities include evaluating student performance and achievement to be documented on report cards and other records. The mean annual salary for elementary school teachers is $44,350.

ART TEACHER

You prepare and teach lessons in art appreciation, art history, and technique. You are responsible for getting the necessary equipment and materials and making sure they are used safely. You encourage students to express their creativity. The mean annual salary for an art teacher is $45,000.

MUSIC TEACHER

You prepare and teach lessons in music appreciation and musicianship. You may even teach certain classes to play a musical instrument, such as the recorder. You must see that your students handle instruments and care from them properly. Other responsibilities may include conducting a student choir, band, or orchestra, accompanying the national anthem and school song at assemblies, and rehearsing with students for plays, graduation, and other events involving music. The mean annual salary for a music teacher is $45,000, although many schools and districts will add on additional fees for each of these additional responsibilities, especially those involving after-school rehearsals.

PHYSICAL EDUCATION TEACHER

You teach and supervise team and individual sports and skills, encourage and discuss physical fitness, and promote safety in exercise. Depending on the size and type of school and the grade levels involved, you may also conduct swimming classes (including lifesaving courses), coach competitive sports teams, and even work with students hoping to be recruited by college teams after graduation. The mean annual salary for a physical education teacher is $45,000, although there may be additional pay for additional responsibilities, such as coaching an extracurricular sport.

SPECIAL EDUCATION TEACHER

You prepare very specialized lessons and teach disabled students with special needs. You may specialize in teaching deaf children, which requires fluency in American Sign Language. You may specialize in teaching learning disabled students, which requires understanding of their condition and proper treatment, as well as special teaching techniques. There are quite a number of sub-specialties in this area, and many are covered by special education licensing. Other responsibilities include conferring with parents and specialists, evaluating student performance and achievement to be documented on report cards and other records, and making recommendations for further intervention. The mean annual salary for special education teachers is $46,790.

SECONDARY SCHOOL (MIDDLE SCHOOL OR HIGH SCHOOL) TEACHER

You prepare lessons and teach adolescent students, usually in just one or two particular subjects. Because you are responsible for teaching a specific academic subject, you have specialized knowledge and expertise in that field. You must also be prepared to deal with teenage behavior, and to build relationships with students you may only see for one classroom period each day. Other responsibilities include evaluating student performance and achievement to be documented on report cards and other records. The mean annual salary for secondary school teachers is $46,000.

READING SPECIALIST

You work individually or with small groups of students who are struggling to read at grade level. You prepare and teach special lessons to help remediate these difficulties and carefully select reading material that is suited to both the student's age and reading level. You consult with classroom teachers, school psychologists, and parents to make appropriate plans and recommendations for each student's special needs, and monitor and report on the student's progress. The mean annual salary for reading specialists is $43,000 in a full-time position, although some schools only offer part-time positions for this specialty.

RELIGIOUS STUDIES TEACHER

You teach in a private religious school, such as a Catholic (parochial) school or Jewish yeshivah. You prepare and teach lessons on religious subjects, such as the Bible, or on languages associated with the religion, such as Latin or Hebrew. You may also teach about holidays, prayers, and other religious matters, and prepare students for various rites and rituals. For certain religious subjects, your school may require you to be a member of the clergy. The mean annual salary for religious studies teachers varies more widely than that for most other teaching specialties because of the diverse types of funding at the schools run by different faiths. While Catholic schools are centrally controlled and receive funding from their local parish, for example, other religions' schools may be independently operated and must rely on other sources of funding. However, you can expect salaries for teachers of religious studies to be commensurate with those of teachers of secular subjects at the same school. Nationwide, the salary range is $35,000 to $55,000, with an average of $47,000. Like salaries in public schools, these numbers will be higher in wealthier communities and lower in financially strapped communities.

SCHOOL LIBRARY/MEDIA SPECIALIST

You manage the school's collection of books and other media. Your responsibilities include maintaining and updating this collection, acquiring new and replacement materials; managing the borrowing program; helping students find materials; and organizing, labeling, and shelving the collection. You may also teach library research skills to older students, and read aloud to younger ones. Finally, you may also be responsible for equipment, such as videocassette players, which can be borrowed by other teachers. The mean annual salary for school library/media specialists is $45,520.

COMPUTER SCIENCE TEACHER

You prepare and teach age-appropriate lessons about computer skills and computer literacy. Topics covered may include keyboarding skills (typing); basic programming; word processing and other software used in the school; and Internet skills, such as research and online safety. You may also moderate an online pen-pal program or student e-groups, and you may also be responsible for maintaining and updating your school's Web site and email server. The mean annual salary for computer science teachers is $48,000.

Careers in School Support and Administration

These are careers for people who are interested in working with children, but not in a classroom full of students. They usually require a master's degree specializing in a particular function, although some do not, while others require a doctorate as well. Many, though not all, require state licensing in the particular specialty, but because state requirements vary so much from state to state and from year to year, it's important to check the latest regulations in your locality.

ATHLETIC DIRECTOR

Schools with very large athletic programs may need to hire numerous physical education teachers and coaches. As athletic director, you are in charge of these teachers and coaches, assigning classes and team coaching responsibilities, supervising the department budget, overseeing the acquisition of equipment and supplies, establishing schedules, and monitoring the maintenance of facilities. You may also need to deal with local media, resolve disputes, and arrange transportation. The mean annual salary for athletic directors is over $80,000.

GUIDANCE COUNSELOR

You provide psychological and/or academic counseling to the students. You may be responsible for psychological, IQ, and achievement testing and assessment; helping students select and apply to high schools or colleges (depending on the grade level of your school); and working with troubled students. You may create special programs, assist during emotionally traumatic events, and refer certain students for outside treatment. In larger and wealthier schools, these responsibilities may be divided between two or more counselors, but in small or financially strapped schools, one person may have to handle all of these tasks. You will have to earn a graduate degree in school psychology or possibly some other relevant field of psychology. The mean average salary for guidance counselors is $45,000.

DEAN OF STUDENTS

Whereas the principal works with superintendents, board members, and other adults as much as with children, you, as dean of students, deal mostly with the children themselves. You oversee both academic and extracurricular activities and help students balance these responsibilities and grow into leadership roles. The mean annual salary for a dean of students is about $75,000.

ADMISSIONS DIRECTOR

You recruit new students by preparing brochures and other literature and by conducting information sessions. You oversee the application process and maintain applicant files, including application forms, test scores, and interviews. Your exact responsibilities may vary, depending on the type of school. For example, private schools often have very competitive admissions, requiring you to scrutinize applicants much more thoroughly, and to be more involved in recruitment and the "courting" of prospective students and their parents. The mean annual salary for admissions directors is $37,000.

SPEECH/LANGUAGE PATHOLOGIST/AUDIOLOGIST

You may also be called a speech therapist or some similar term. You work with students who have speech defects or language deficits, often but not always due to hearing problems. You assess students for trouble in these areas, try to determine the cause, and recommend a course of intervention. Mild problems can be resolved in speech therapy sessions with you during school hours, while severe problems may require medical attention, such as medication, hearing aids, or even surgery. You will need a master's degree in this specialty to meet state licensing requirements. The mean annual salary for speech/language pathologists and audiologists is $60,000, although many schools only offer part-time positions.

PRINCIPAL

You oversee virtually everything that goes on in your school. You have the final say in hiring faculty, implementing new programs, and upgrading the school's facilities and equipment. You manage the teachers, allocate resources, and moderate disputes. You represent the school to inquiring parents, the board of education or directors, and the community at large, and must appear at meetings and conferences in this role. You will have to get a graduate degree in school administration in order to become a school principal. The mean annual salary for school principals is close to $80,000, although it varies according to the type of school (public, private, or religious).

SCHOOL SOCIAL WORKER

You work with the school to provide needed services for troubled, disabled, and at-risk children. This may involve testing, consulting with parents and guardians, reporting to outside agencies, and making referrals. Many of these responsibilities overlap with those of a guidance counselor or school psychologist. However, you are particularly equipped to deal with larger crises affecting a student, such as child abuse and neglect, homelessness, and foster care. You will need to earn a graduate degree in social work. The mean annual salary for social workers is around $48,000.

SUPERINTENDENT OF SCHOOLS

You are responsible for a school district's goals, strategies, and policies. Goals may include getting more students to read at grade level or to graduate on time. Strategies are district-wide techniques for achieving goals, such as setting aside funding, placing specialists in each school, or adopting a new series of textbooks. Policies are rules that enable goals and strategies to be carried out, such as encouraging multi-ethnic cooperation or zero-tolerance of violent behavior. You will also be called upon to deal with problems involving a school principal or more than one school in your district. Diplomacy and conflict resolution skills are critical here. You will probably need to earn a doctorate in education. The mean annual salary for school superintendents is $80,000.

Careers Outside of Schools

These are careers in education for people who are not employees of a school. Some involve working for other industries and businesses, while others can be done in private practice. Salaries given do not represent private practice earnings, which may fluctuate.

EDUCATION CONSULTANT

You advise schools and government representatives on educational policies. You may design special programs, including training for in-service teachers and administrators. You help assess and recommend curriculum for schools. You may specialize in a particular subject area, a certain grade level (such as early childhood), or a special needs population, although you may also be a generalist. You will need to have at least a master's degree. The mean annual salary for education consultants is $90,000.

EDUCATION RESEARCHER

You conduct research on educational technology and strategy, on how students learn and behave, and other matters of concern to educators. You may research the effectiveness of a new program or teaching method. You will design the research, observe and collect data, analyze statistics, and write up a final report. Your employer may be a school district, university or state education department, a private institution, or an educational publisher. You may even do research independently with grant funding. You may begin as an assistant to a more senior researcher and work your way up, perhaps earning a graduate degree in statistics or another related field. The mean annual salary for educational researchers is $55,000, although many researchers are hired by the project.

PROGRAM/CURRICULUM DESIGNER

You design educational programs and materials, using your knowledge and training to determine the best way to present the subject matter to the target audience. You must consider the goal of the program or curriculum, the age and education level of the learners, the best way to make the material comprehensible and interesting, and the amount of review and practice needed, all the while considering budget restraints, media availability, and timing. This may be as simple as choosing a combination of textbooks or as complex as designing a multi-media teaching unit from scratch. The mean annual salary can vary widely, depending on your type of employer and your own education and experience.

PUBLIC HEALTH EDUCATOR

You design and implement programs to educate the public about important health issues. Your goal is to raise awareness in the community so that people will know how to better take care of themselves and their families. You may do this by conducting workshops, designing pamphlets, or developing public service advertisements. Your audience may be people in a particular life stage, such as teenagers or the elderly; people with a particular condition, such as diabetics or allergy sufferers; people who are coping with a special experience, such as veterans or pregnant women, or even the general public during an epidemic. You may be employed by a hospital, a government health department, the Veterans' Administration, a social services agency, or an organization serving a particular population. Examples of health issues of concern today include AIDS prevention and obesity. The mean annual salary for public health educators is $58,000.

PRIVATE TUTOR

You work one-on-one or in small groups with students who need additional, remedial, or make-up lessons in a particular subject. Your students may need help because they are struggling with the same material in the regular classroom or because they have missed classes for some reason and need to make up the work. Gifted and talented students may be interested in honing their skills or learning more about a particular subject than the classroom teacher can offer, and transfer students may need temporary help to catch up to their classmates. You may be employed by the school, by a community center or other program that offers after-school services, or by one of the growing number of commercial tutoring centers, or you may offer your services privately. Salaries vary widely depending on your type of employment. Tutors working through a college help center often make less than $20 an hour because they are being paid by the students. Tutors working privately in middle- to upper-class communities are paid by the parents and can command fees of $50 to $90 an hour! Tutors working through a school system or commercial center earn more than college tutors but less than independent tutors, and are paid according to scales set up in accordance with union or other guidelines.

TEXTBOOK AND CHILDREN'S BOOK WRITER/EDITOR

You write and/or edit books aimed at students. These books may be very structured textbooks with accompanying workbooks or practice pages, or they may simply be literature aimed at children. In addition to writing or editing an age-appropriate manuscript, you may help to decide on illustrations, graphics, and other design issues. As a writer, your pay depends on your current contract, which in turn takes into consideration your experience, expertise in the subject, projected sales, and other variables. Typically, authors may receive an advance of $2,000 to $13,000 and 5% to 15% of the royalties the book earns. The mean annual salary for editors is $59,000.

INDUSTRIAL TRAINER

You train and retrain a company's employees in skills they need for their jobs. These skills may include operating machinery, speaking a foreign language, computer literacy, and so forth. The company may have its own training center where you can teach these skills, or the company may send those in need of training to a hotel or other meeting facility.

You may be employed by a company, especially if the nature of the business and job turnover require constant training, or you may work as a private contractor. Either way, you consult with the company about its training needs and report back on the success of the training program, modifying it as needed. The mean annual salary for experienced industrial trainers is $80,000.

Overseas and Volunteer Teaching Opportunities

As an American, you may be interested in teaching in a foreign country if:

◆ You are interested in spending some time in a foreign country but need to earn a living while doing so

◆ You are not sure if you really want to devote your career to teaching, and want a relatively short-term job to see if you like it

◆ You will be living in a foreign country for a limited time due to family reasons, such as a spouse's job, and you would like something to do while you're there

It is unusual for American citizens to continue teaching in a foreign country for the duration of their career, although there are always exceptions. Generally, these exceptions involve people who are either working for an American institution, such as the military or a corporation, or people who have gone through the process of becoming trained and licensed to teach according to the regulations of whichever nation they are in. The latter, however, is beyond the scope of this book, as each nation (and sometimes provinces, states, or cities within the nation) has its own requirements. If you are interested in becoming qualified to teach in another country, a good place to start looking for the information you need is at that country's local embassy.

If you are interested in a shorter-term teaching assignment overseas, your American qualifications may be accepted, especially if you work through an organization that already has arrangements in place with foreign governments. In such cases, the government in question will accept the organization's investigation of your qualifications, knowing that the organization has appropriate standards.

Other good sources of information include professors of foreign languages or who have overseas connections, periodicals aimed at foreign or ethnic groups in the United States, and many job search engines.

THE PEACE CORPS

This well-known organization recruits volunteers to work in communities around the world, providing services ranging from education to health care to business development. People who join the program as teachers may teach a specific subject, such as English, at the elementary, secondary, or college level. They may also train local residents to become teachers themselves.

For some of these jobs, an education degree isn't required, although it can help. Instead, you may be required to have a degree in the subject you will be teaching, such as math or science. But you are also required to have teaching experience, even if it's informal or in the form of tutoring. If you have completed a major in education, you should have all of these requirements fulfilled in the process.

If you would like to train new teachers in your assigned community, you *will* need to have a degree in education, because you will be imparting teaching methods, classroom management, and other relevant skills.

The Peace Corps offers many different kinds of support to its volunteers. It provides three months of initial training and ongoing training throughout the period of service. Many of the skills and experiences acquired this way can be applied to subsequent employment, which is one reason Peace Corps experience looks so good on a resume.

After completing a stint with the Peace Corps, volunteers can get help with job placement through the organization's network, newsletters, and workshops. After two years with the Peace Corps, volunteers are also given special advantages when seeking Federal employment.

In addition, the Peace Corps, in cooperation with many American colleges and universities, offers scholarship and tuition reduction programs for former volunteers who go back to school for master's or advanced degrees.

Peace Corps volunteers receive financial benefits in three ways: pay and living expenses (based on the cost of living in the particular region where you will be working), including housing, medical care, and transportation; transitional funds of over $6,000 to help former volunteers readjust to life back home; and deferment of student loans.

For more information about Peace Corps teaching opportunities, visit www.peacecorps.gov. The Web site can also direct you to regional offices and representatives on campus who can give you more information.

TEACH CORPS

A private organization placing American and Canadian college graduates in overseas English teaching positions, this company specializes in working with private language schools in Asian nations. This frees the teachers from having to fulfill foreign licensing requirements, and the company provides training in methods of teaching English. The organization screens both the teachers and the participating schools to ensure a smooth transition and a comfortable fit.

A degree in education is not required, although it certainly provides you an advantage.

As in the Peace Corps, salary and benefits are based on the cost of living in the place where you are assigned. Furthermore, the salaries are paid in local currency, the value of which changes with the exchange rate. For example, teachers in Seoul are paid approximately 2 million *won* per month, which currently is around $1,500. Teachers throughout China, however, are paid approximately 3,200 *yuan* per month, which is only about $400. However, the cost of living, including food, medical care, and transportation, is so much less in China that one can live quite comfortably on this salary.

For more information about Teach Corps, visit www.teachcorps.com.

TEACH FOR AMERICA

This relatively new organization is part of the AmeriCorps national service network. It was set up to help overcome educational inequities in impoverished American communities, both urban and rural. Volunteers sign up to teach for two years in a school that meets the organization's standards.

Participating teachers must be college graduates, but do not have to be education majors or licensed teachers. The No Child Left Behind

Act allows schools to hire uncertified teachers who meet the qualifications for local alternative certification, and Teach For America's summer training programs allow candidates to fulfill these requirements before the school year begins. In many states, this experience qualifies teachers to become fully certified, although some states may require additional course work.

Teachers receive training and related support from Teach For America, but are paid directly by the school system to which they are assigned. Salaries range from $22,000 to $41,000, depending on the pay scale of the given locale. Teach For America and AmeriCorps provide additional money in the form of interest-free loans, transitional expenses, and an education award, which can be used to pay off college loans or go on for a graduate degree.

For more information about Teach For America, including participating schools and on-campus recruitment, visit www.teachfor america.org.

Chapter 6

Breaking into the Job Market

This chapter looks at where to go to apply for teacher certification and licensure. It also explores some of the ways you can apply your degree to a career in education, including the following:

◆ Teaching grade, middle, and high school

◆ Becoming a principal or superintendent

◆ Becoming a teaching specialist

This chapter also provides tips on searching for jobs if you have determined that you don't want to teach, but still want to pursue a career in education. Finally, the chapter concludes with some tips on how to land a job in your desired career by preparing you for job interviews.

Getting Certified in Your State

In general, you'll need to be certified if you want to teach in a school setting. Your college advisor and peer group can usually help you navigate when and where you take certification tests. Certification differs by state, and each state has its own certification process and home office. You'll need to check the certification requirements in the state you'll be teaching in.

Alabama
Web site: www.alsde.edu/general/general_certification_
information.pdf
Phone: 334-242-9977

Alaska
Web site: www.eed.state.ak.us/TeacherCertification
Phone: 907-465-2831

Arizona
Web site: www.ade.state.az.us/certification
Phone: 602-542-4367

Arkansas
Web site: Arkedu.state.ar.us/teachers
Phone: 501-682-4342

California
Web site: www.cta.ca.gov
Phone: 916-445-7524

Colorado
Web site: www.cde.state.co.us/index_license.htm
Phone: 303-866-6628

Connecticut
Web site: www.ctcrt.org
Phone: 860-713-6969

Delaware
Web site: Deeds.doe.state.de.us
Phone: 888-759-9133

District of Columbia
Web site: www.teachdc.org
Phone: 202-442-5377

Florida
Web site: www.fldoe.org/edcert
Phone: 850-488-2317/800-445-6739

Georgia
Web site: www.gapsc.com
Phone: 404-232-2500 (metro Atlanta)/800-869-7775 (elsewhere)

Hawaii
Web site: www.htsb.org
Phone: 808-586-2600

Idaho
Web site: www.sde.state.id.us/certification
Phone: 208-332-6880

Illinois
Web site: www.isbe.net/teachers
Phone: 866-262-6663 (Springfield)/312-814-2220 (Chicago)

Indiana
Web site: www.in.gov/psb
Phone: 866-542-3672

Iowa
Web site: www.state.ia.us/boee
Phone: 515-281-3245

Kansas
Web site: www.ksde.org/cert/cert.html
Phone: 785-291-3678

Kentucky
Web site: www.kyepsb.net
Phone: 888-598-7667

Louisiana
Web site: www.doe.state.la.us/lde/tsac/home.html
Phone: 877-453-2721

Maine
Web site: www.state.me.us/education/cert/cert.htm
Phone: 207-624-6603

Maryland
Web site: www.certification.msde.state.md.us
Phone: 410-767-0412

Massachusetts
Web site: www.doe.mass.edu/educators/e_license.html
Phone: 781-338-6600

Michigan
Web site: www.michigan.gov/mde
Phone: 517-373-3310

Minnesota
Web site: www.education.state.mn.us/html/intro_licensure.htm
Phone: 651-582-8691

Mississippi
Web site: www.mde.k12.ms.us/license
Phone: 601-359-3483

Missouri
Web site: www.dese.mo.gov/divteachqual/teachcert
Phone: 573-751-0051/573-751-3847

Montana
Web site: www.opi.state.mt.us/cert/index.html
Phone: 406-444-3150

Nebraska
Web site: www.nde.state.ne.us/tcert/tcert.html
Phone: 402-471-2496 (forms)/402-471-0739

Nevada
Web site: www.nde.state.nv.us/licensure
Phone: 702-486-6458 (Las Vegas)/775-687-9115 (Carson City)

New Hampshire
Web site: www.ed.state.nh.us/education/doe/organization/
programsupport/boc.htm
Phone: 603-271-3872/603-271-3874

New Jersey
Web site: www.state.nj.us/njded/educators/license
Phone: 603-292-2070

New Mexico
Web site: www.sde.state.nm.us/div/ais/lic/index.html
Phone: 505-827-6587

New York
Web site: www.highered.nysed.gov/tcert
Phone: 518-474-3901

North Carolina
Web site: www.dpi.state.nc.us/licensure
Phone: 919-807-3300

North Dakota
Web site: www.state.nd.us/espb
Phone: 701-328-2264

Ohio
Web site: www.ode.state.oh.us/teaching-profession/teacher/
certification_licensure
Phone: 614-466-3593

Oklahoma
Web site: www.sde.state.ok.us/pro/tcert/profstd.html
Phone: 405-521-3337

Oregon
Web site: www.tspc.state.or.us
Phone: 503-378-3586

Pennsylvania
Web site: www.teaching.state.pa.us/teaching
Phone: 717-787-3356

Rhode Island
Web site: www.ridoe.net/teacher_cert
Phone: 401-222-4600

South Carolina
Web site: www.scteachers.org
Phone: 877-885-5280 (SC)/803-734-8466 (elsewhere)

South Dakota
Web site: www.state.sd.us/deca/OPA
Phone: 605-773-3553

Tennessee
Web site: www.state.tn.us/education/lic_home
Phone: 615-532-4885 (forms)/615-532-4873

Texas
Web site: www.sbec.state.tx.us/SBECOnline
Phone: 888-863-5880

Utah
Web site: www.usoe.k12.ut.us/cert
Phone: 801-538-7740

Vermont
Web site: www.state.vt.us/educ/new/html/maincert.html
Phone: 802-828-2445

Virginia
Web site: www.pen.k12.va.us/VDOE/newvdoe/teached.html
Phone: 804-692-0157

Washington
Web site: www.k12.wa.us/certification
Phone: 360-725-6400

West Virginia
Web site: http://wvde.state.wv.us/certification
Phone: 800-982-2378

Wisconsin
Web site: www.dpi.state.wi.us/dpi/dlsis/tel
Phone: 800-266-1027

Wyoming
Web site: www.k12.wy.us/ptsb
Phone: 800-675-6893 (WY)/307-777-7291 (elsewhere)

Finding a Job as a Grade, Middle, or High School Teacher

So you've received your degree that may or may not include a teaching certificate. Now what? It's time to take the next step toward your career by initiating your job search.

Where to begin? What about the school where you student taught? If you enjoyed your experience there and, more important, the school's administrators and cooperating teachers were impressed with your attitude and your work with students, you might end up with a job offer.

If your experience at the school where you student taught was less than pleasurable, or perhaps you accidentally put a dent in the school superintendent's new sports car in the school parking lot, relax. There are other resources available.

The most obvious place for a grade, middle, and high school teacher to begin a job search is through the college placement office. Depending on the size of your school, you should be aware that members of the placement staff usually are very busy helping students. This means that although you can get their help, you'll need to be active in your job search as well.

Don't underestimate the Internet and newspaper employment sections as sources for job openings. Remember that there's a very high turnover in the education professions, and sometimes school districts are desperate to fill vacant positions. The quickest way to reach job seekers is through the want ads and such Internet job search engines as monster.com.

Finding a Job as a Principal or Superintendent

If you're an education major who wishes to become a principal or superintendent, you'll have a lengthier road to travel. The typical price of entry into these career paths is an advanced degree. Once you have your advanced degree in hand, however, you'll need to work yourself up the career ladder to your desired position.

Almost all principals have a master's degree. In addition, every state requires principals to acquire a license in school administration.

If you desire to become a principal, chances are you'll begin your professional career as an assistant principal. Take the opportunity as an assistant principal to learn as much as you can; you'll receive some invaluable on-the-job training. You'll be able to take these observations to your job interviews for subsequent principal positions.

Superintendents are another story. Most superintendents began their careers as teachers, before moving on as assistant principals and principals. If you wish to become a superintendent, you'll need good contacts, as many superintendents are hired from within the school district.

Finding a Job as a Specialist

Specialist careers include English as a second language teacher, school counselor, coach, adult education teacher, media specialist, librarian, and special education teacher. Begin your search just as if you were seeking a regular grade school, middle school, or high school position—by putting together reference letters, a portfolio, and placement folder, and going to your college's placement office. (For more on these steps, see the section "Job Searching Skills" later in this chapter.)

It's a good idea to find someone who is already in the career you wish to pursue. This individual can give you good tips on how they prepared for the career. They can also tell you about internships, professional organizations, or informal networking opportunities that you can explore to benefit your career.

Specialists typically either have or are working toward advanced degrees. If you are in this situation, you will be able to interact with other people with similar career goals—and professors who are in regular contact with school districts that might be looking for someone with your special skill set. As you narrow your career choices down, the size of your classes decreases proportionally. This gives you a chance to strike up a closer relationship with the professors who can help guide you toward your first professional job.

Once again, never underestimate Web-based employment sites and newspaper want ads in your job search. Many school districts use these media to advertise openings.

Many specialist jobs—such as library, media, and computer lab specialists—will require you to teach. But what if you decided that teaching students isn't what you want to do? There are plenty of jobs in education that don't require you to teach, and you should have no trouble finding an interviewer who understands that you wish to pursue a career outside of the classroom. A tactful method of handling such a delicate issue, however, is recommended. If asked during an interview why you prefer not to teach, be prepared with a thoughtful and honest answer. Stress that your skills are better applied to curriculum or administration, for example, rather than leading a classroom.

Finding a Job as a Corporate Trainer

In the past two decades, corporate training has become more prevalent. Many Fortune 500 companies require that their employees receive a certain amount of training each year. Sometimes this training is done online, but there are other companies that either send their employees to seminars or bring corporate trainers in-house to train employees.

Many corporate trainers come from teaching backgrounds, but that is not always the case. Some trainers discover a penchant for teaching while in their professional career. But as an education major, you have a distinct advantage in this arena: You understand education methodologies and have had experience standing in front of a classroom and explaining concepts. For those with an education major who decide teaching in the schools isn't for them, corporate training can be a great way to mesh an interest in education with a different type of position.

Some major companies hire public relations and communications companies to train their field personnel. For example, the automotive industry regularly asks the agencies that they hire to set up training for their warehousing and distribution, dealership, and repair shop employees. Many of these jobs require a well-rounded knowledge of a specific business, however, and can require a bit of extra preparation. If you're thinking corporate training might be a good fit for your skills, the following ideas might help you get a foot in the door:

1. Identify the industry in the area where you'd like to work. This could be automotive, insurance, software, and so on.

2. Familiarize yourself with the major issues confronting the industry. This will take some research, although you can do much of it online through online journals, message boards, and even company Web sites. This is important because today's corporate and manufacturing environments are extremely competitive and faced with such economic realities as outsourcing, fuel and material prices, healthcare and pension costs, foreign competition, and government policies. The more you know about these issues, the more convincing you'll be when you interview for a corporate training position. Company human resource professionals will look favorably on a potential employee who is sympathetic to the challenges facing their industry. You'll also be doing yourself a favor by distinguishing yourself from other interviewees with your added knowledge.

3. When you contact the human resources department of a company in the industry you're interested in working in, ask whether they do their training with in-house corporate trainers, or if they contract their training with outside companies that service the training needs of that industry. If it's the former, ask the representative if the company has any openings. If it's the latter, tactfully ask the representative if he or she can give you the name of the company that provides corporate training.

Job Searching Skills

Unless you're incredibly lucky and someone offers you a position as you step down from the podium with your diploma, you're going to need to buckle down to land your first job. Now that you're in the hunt for a job, you'll need to familiarize yourself with the job search resources available to you, as well as what you can do to market yourself to prospective employers—both before and during an interview.

PLACEMENT SERVICES

Placement services are businesses that help job seekers. Most charge a fee for membership. In exchange for a fee, the placement service provides a list of job openings and contact information.

Before trying a placement service off campus, visit your college placement office. Remember, it is in your college's best interest to place as many of its graduates as it can. The more students the college places in the students' chosen careers, the better the college looks when recruiting new students.

When you talk to your college placement counselor, he or she will advise you on how to open a placement file. A placement file is a folder that should include letters of recommendation from both personal and professional sources, a resume, and any other information that would be of interest to a prospective employer.

If you are dissatisfied with the results of your job search through your college's placement office, there are other resources you can turn to before resorting to an independent, for-profit placement service that can charge hundreds of dollars. For example, teacher's unions and state education departments are two good places to turn to during any education job search—and both are either inexpensive or free. Both maintain job boards in all aspects of education—not just teaching. You can find where the union and education departments are located by searching the Internet or asking in the Education Department of your college.

REFERENCES AND LETTERS OF RECOMMENDATION

A good placement file will include contact information for references. References are people with whom you've had a professional relationship.

Employers will want to contact your references to ask questions about your character, your dependability, and other such questions. So make sure you give the most accurate contact information for your references. You'll want to ask potential references if they are willing to talk to your potential employers. Many employers require at least three references. Good sources of references are the principal or teacher you worked with during your student teaching, professors familiar with your work, and former employers—especially if the job (such as a camp counselor) can translate well to the positions you'll be applying for.

You also will be well served by having solid letters of recommendation in your placement file. These letters send a clear message to potential employers—that you have displayed professionalism in your chosen field or during your academic career and will make a good employee. These letters should come from professors in your education major or minor, as well as mentors or individuals who worked with you during your internships or student teaching. Employers may want to see three letters of recommendation as they consider you for a position.

When soliciting references or letters of recommendation, be sure to let the people you're soliciting know that you're not campaigning for a Nobel Prize in education. The references and letters should offer clear and concise descriptions of your academic achievements; talents; professional and personal demeanor; and such skills as the ability to deal with stressful situations, deadlines, and other people. Encourage your references to be honest and assure them that you will not see what they have written.

PORTFOLIOS

Many schools require students to keep a portfolio. This is a good idea whether or not your college requires it. Your portfolio is an excellent way to show prospective employers your best work.

A portfolio varies from person to person, depending on student-teaching or internship experience and area of concentration. A complete portfolio provides examples of your professional skills from several different angles.

A portfolio can be put together in separate formats. If most of what you want to display to potential employers consists of written materials, a portfolio can be a three-ring binder. If your portfolio contains artwork for a bulletin board, you may require an artist's portfolio.

When putting together your portfolio, consider including the following:

◆ Classroom curriculum or lesson plans that you have put together for your student-teaching assignment or internship

◆ Photographs, DVDs, or videotapes of you "in action" as a student teacher or intern

◆ Testimonials from your cooperating teacher, professors, or internship supervisor

Because the portfolio is such an important tool, make sure you spend as much time as you can on it. It should be neat, well organized, clean, and easily accessible. Your portfolio should tell your story in such a way that you are presented as the best-qualified and best-prepared teacher for the job opening for which you're applying. If you're an elementary education major, it may be difficult to avoid cuteness—especially if showing samples of your bulletin board work—but for most education majors it's best to maintain as much of a professional, no-nonsense image as possible when displaying your work. Don't worry about clever titles for your portfolio, either. A cover page or title lettering on the cover should identify simply that this is your portfolio.

Interviewing

So you landed an interview at a place where you'd really like to be employed. Remember that first impressions go a long way during an interview—if you make a bad impression, you may not be asked back for a second interview, much less be offered the position. The following tips may help you place yourself at the top of the hiring school's list:

◆ **Research the school, business, and area.** The more you know about a potential employer before your interview, the better prepared you'll be with important questions. This step will show that you're serious enough about the position to have done your homework. Look for information on the Web, by talking to other people in the area, or by searching local newspapers.

◆ **Good Grooming.** Wear clean, unwrinkled clothing, and make sure your hair, skin, and fingernails are clean. If you're a man with facial hair, make sure your beard and/or mustache are trimmed.

◆ **Dress Respectably.** You may not have an expensive suit of Italian silk, but dress yourself in a dignified fashion—nothing too casual or too formal. If you're a man, wear either a business suit and tie or a sport coat, tie, and dress slacks. If you're a woman, wear a business suit that may consist of either slacks or a skirt with a blazer, a modest blouse and skirt, or a modest dress. Too tight or too short clothing on men and women sends the wrong signals to an interviewer.

◆ **Arrive Rested.** You may have been able to pull all-nighters in college before the big test, but a job interview requires you to be on the top of your game. Proper rest ensures that your mental engine is firing on all cylinders.

◆ **Come Prepared.** You'll make a bad impression immediately if you arrive at an interview without a copy of your resume, your portfolio, and a pen and pad of paper for taking notes. Before going to the interview, write a list of questions you'd like answered during the interview; this preparedness shows the interviewer that you're organized, serious about your career, and genuinely in charge of all aspects of your professional and personal life.

◆ **Keep Personal Details to a Minimum.** Talk only about yourself in terms of what you'll bring to the classroom or workplace. Don't dwell on topics that include where you grew up or outside hobbies and relationships.

◆ **Be Courteous.** Obviously you'll want to display good manners while on the interview. Also be aware that nervous or shy behavior may be interpreted as rudeness; if you're feeling nervous, speak slowly so that you don't inadvertently blurt out something that can be interpreted as inappropriate. Follow social protocol by shaking hands, by referring to someone as Mr. or Ms. until given permission to use the interviewer's first name, and by never interrupting the person interviewing you.

◆ **Be Conscientious.** Watch your interviewer's reactions. If his or her eyes start to wander, your answers may be too long and you could be losing the interviewer's attention. If you perceive that one of your answers wasn't understood, ask whether your answer made sense. If not, politely rephrase your response in a more concise fashion.

◆ **Be Honest.** Dishonesty is never a positive trait, but lying during an interview is the biggest no-no in the professional world. Being caught in a lie is immediate grounds for being turned down for a job. If you're hired after lying during your interview (or on your resume), you may be dismissed once your dishonesty is discovered. During the interview, put a positive spin on your experience and skills, but don't be dishonest about them.

◆ **Follow Up.** Send your interviewer a handwritten thank-you note to thank him or her for their time. You may also use this opportunity to address an important point that you might've forgotten or under-emphasized during the interview.

Chapter 7

Case Studies

Natalie, an Author
WHAT I USED TO DO AND WHAT I DO NOW

love books. I originally wanted to get a degree in library science. I started out as an English major, hoping to parlay that into the library program, but then I got married and started a family, and I couldn't balance raising children with commuting to the campus where I would have had to go. But when my children were old enough to go to school, I went back for a master's degree as a reading specialist and started teaching in a school near where we lived. After a while, one of the local colleges wanted me to work on a new reading program, but unfortunately, the budget was cut and the program couldn't be implemented. So the college offered me a job teaching adolescent psychology instead, even though that wasn't even my specialty. I handled it by inviting different guest speakers to the class over the course of the semester, including professionals who worked with adolescents as well as a group of my teenaged son's classmates, so that the college class could meet directly with this age group.

After my children grew up and went off on their own, my husband and I decided to give up our big house and move to a nice apartment in the city, so I took early retirement from the school system and thought about what I'd like to do next. While I was thinking, I helped open a bookstore for children with my daughter and a friend of hers. We made it into a fun place for children so that they would grow to love reading as I do, with comfortable places for kids to sit and look at books, and special events to draw the crowds in and get them excited.

Based on my experience as a retired schoolteacher, I began tutoring in my new community. I found a lot of young people needed help developing good study skills. It's shocking how little schools do to help students learn how to learn! Often, kids will be able to wing it for a few years, but really get into trouble in middle and high school when the work is harder and there's more to juggle. In addition to some of the typical academic subjects, I also found a bit of a niche for myself working with students who found themselves in this type of situation.

After a while, I felt ready to spread my wings and do some learning of my own. I didn't want to go back to classroom teaching at this point in my life, but I did want to be able to share the things I discovered. Someone suggested that with my teaching skills and the research and writing skills that go along with them, I could write non-fiction books. That would allow me to combine several of the things I enjoy: researching, writing, and communicating with young people.

Now I write biography and history books aimed at young adults. Because my readers are students, I am very careful to do thorough research and to include a lot of extras to help them get a better handle on the subject, such as timelines, family trees, diagrams, and lists for further reading.

When I prepare to write a book, my research can take me on wonderful adventures. Sometimes I get to travel to interesting places to see where the person I'm writing about lived and worked. I've gotten special permission to go into restricted library archives to read letters, journals, and other documents that were written very long ago. It's quite a feeling to touch a letter that was written 200 years ago!

I also have to develop some expertise in peripheral matters related to whatever I'm writing about, and that can be fun (though sometimes distracting!). I need to learn about how people lived in earlier times: how they dressed, what kind of music they listened to, what ideas and ideals they believed in, and so forth. If I'm writing about someone who lived before the age of photography, I have to find paintings or drawings of the person, which can mean a trip to a museum or gallery.

WHY I CHOSE THE EDUCATION MAJOR

Teaching was a popular choice among educated women when I was in college. If you wanted or needed to work outside the home, it was a respectable job that called for traits women were said to have, such as dealing with children, and the workday ended in time for you to get your husband's dinner on the table. For me, it also meant that I could be home when my own children were home from school, both on a daily basis and during vacations. A common wisdom for women of my generation was that a teaching license was the perfect safety net in case something happened to your husband or his job.

I've always tended to be very detail-oriented, so the administrative parts of being a teacher came naturally to me. I learned pretty quickly how important it is to prepare lesson materials thoroughly so that students can really get a lot out of it. Not only does that help the kids learn better, but I like to think it also earned me a lot more respect. My students could see that I had gone to a lot of effort, and it motivated them to respond in kind.

HOW THE EDUCATION MAJOR PREPARED ME FOR MY JOB

As an author, the education major helped me learn to do several important things. The first is, of course, how to teach, by which I mean how to present information to students in the right way to get their interest and help them understand and integrate the knowledge they're picking up.

The second important skill I learned was writing. Obviously, a writer has to know how to communicate ideas clearly without being boring. When you're writing for young people, there are added concerns. You have to be aware of the level of vocabulary you can use, what types of facts they can comprehend, what has to be explained in more detail, and how to get them interested in what you have to say. Of course, these are considerations when writing for adults as well, but they really take on a whole new level with young audiences. The lessons I learned as an education student prepared me to deal with these issues.

A third skill is how to do research. I've always loved to read, so my college library was a treasure-trove for me, and learning how to prepare for a term paper or exam taught me how to conduct an efficient "treasure hunt!"

A fourth skill is time management. As a college student, I had to learn to juggle all the different courses I was taking, each with its own homework, exams, and due dates. As a teacher, I had to learn to allot sufficient time in my classroom for different lessons and activities, and this was one of the things taught in my education classes. Now, when I write books, I have to set aside time for research, phone calls, rewrites, and so many other tasks, and I'm able to do this because of what I learned in college.

A fifth skill is public speaking. Although I'm no longer standing in front of a class every day and addressing students, I am often called upon to speak at schools, libraries, and other institutions about my books and related topics. In addition to being invited to be a guest lecturer, I've also appeared on scholarly panels with some well-known experts. This would have been particularly nerve-racking if I hadn't learned to speak clearly, professionally, and confidently, as I did to become a teacher.

OTHER TRAINING

I think a lot of my life experience has served as good training. In addition to teaching, I also had the experience of raising my children and seeing how they changed from one year to the next, so I feel knowledgeable about kids of all ages, not just the grade levels I taught. Helping my kids with homework and studying made me see the learning process from both sides, and they kept me aware of how young people feel about things. Now my grandchildren do the same thing! Each of my children, and now grandchildren, has his or her own special interests and abilities; to keep up with all of them, I've had to stay on my toes, and I think that has expanded my outlook and made me interested in so many different topics. That in itself is great training for an author.

Early on in my adult life, I did have some experience working at one of the leading public libraries in my region. This gave me a lot of valuable experience doing research and tracking down information. And because a lot of the patrons who asked me for help were working on some sort of school project, whether they were elementary school children or graduate students, I found that I had to be very thorough— their grades as well as their understanding depended on it. This is a discipline that I've carried into the way I write my books. I may not be there myself if a young reader has further questions, so I want to make sure there are enough resources in the books I write so that youngsters will know where to look it up independently.

I mentioned time management and organization as a skill I learned in college, but it's also something you get better at over the course of your life. Running a household and raising children, each of whom is off in a different direction, really forces you to get organized! You have to learn which tasks can be put off for a while, when to hand off a job to someone else, and when to say, "I'm sorry, but I just can't do this now."

HELPFUL MOVES

I'll admit that some of the helpful moves in my experience were rather serendipitous. When my husband and I bought our apartment in the city, it just happened to be virtually across the street from a historical society library where I did a lot of my research. A wonderful museum was just blocks away. Now, of course, the Internet allows me to "visit" far away places from my own desk, but having all those resources practically in my lap really got me going in the beginning.

I strongly recommend involving the people around you. When I first set out to write a book, it was largely possible because of my husband's support. We discussed what I wanted to do, and he's learned to respect my time and my work area, and to help out around the house. One of my children grew up to become an expert in a field that has helped me with my research, and I cherish being able to confer together on my books. And of course, so many people have been able to provide me with an "in"—from someone who recommended an agent to a young lady who got me a visitor's pass to her university's library!

PITFALLS TO AVOID

One of my more amusing pitfalls is getting sidetracked when doing research. It's one thing to pick up knowledge about life in the era I'm writing about, but I've caught myself getting completely engrossed in a book about a composer who was popular at that time when I was supposed to be researching a different person altogether. A little of this is understandable, and perhaps unavoidable, but you have to stay focused, or else you'll never finish writing your book!

Remember the importance of time management. You have to map out when to do research and when you'll be ready to write it up, but you also have to remember to stop for lunch. Don't neglect yourself or the people in your life.

When you do research, avoid some of the common pitfalls. Keep in mind that there are often several conflicting versions of something that happened, and as a careful researcher, you'll need to study as many as you can to draw your own conclusion, or at least to be honest enough in your writing to describe the controversy.

What I Love About My Job

My work gives me entrée to a lot of people and places that I wouldn't have otherwise. I've been able to get private tours of places that are off-limits to the public. I've also had the opportunity to meet with scholars and even celebrities who are hard to get an appointment with. I've even gotten permission to look at private or restricted archives and artifacts. I've seen such wonderful people, places, and things, and I really do love that about my job.

A lot of my personal relationships have been rekindled or recast because of my work. I love to include family members in my work. When I travel out of town to visit historical sites, my husband has often come along for the trip, and we've had some wonderful times together. Sometimes, when I'm doing more local research, at a museum, for instance, I can take one of my grandchildren along and make a day trip out of it. Even discussing my research with my children has helped me see them as adults and professionals in their own right, and has brought our parent-child relationship to a whole new level. Lately, some of my older grandchildren are participating in these discussions in a more adult manner than I was ready for!

Things on the Job I Could Do Without

A lot of the things that bother me can be summed up as bureaucracy. I've had editors who made requests that I thought were unreasonable or publishing houses with silly—and conflicting—regulations about how to do things. Fortunately, I've reached the point in my career when I can find editors and publishers I'm comfortable working with. I've had ridiculous experiences doing research, trying to get through red tape, or arriving at a library that was closed when I was told it would be open, or not being allowed in altogether because I had my driver's license with me for identification but not my passport! Some institutions ask for exorbitant fees just to get a parking pass or use the copy machine, and then I have to find out if my publisher will cover the expense.

Then there are those things that just can't be helped, like the blizzard that forces a trip to be cancelled, or the computer that crashes, or the bout of carpal-tunnel syndrome.

Of course, as an author, I have to mention the critics! I've been thrilled with the positive reviews I've gotten, whether it's from a professional book critic in the newspaper or from the teenager down the block. And I was prepared for the fact that not everyone would automatically like everything I put into a book. One critic even said all my charts and tables were "excessive" and distracting! It's one thing to have an opinion, but it's completely frustrating when a reviewer misses the point. My readers include students who may be using my books for research papers, and the information that critic found excessive may be a big help to students. And of course the subjects I write about have their controversial sides, and some critics read entirely too much into my take on these issues, accusing me of all kinds of political leanings and ulterior motives if I take a particular position, or of glossing over the issue if I choose not to delve into it too deeply in a book that, after all, is written for minors!

MY WORK AND MY LIFE

This type of work is a blessing at this point in my life. I have a home office where I keep my computer and research material, with a special phone line for business-related calls, and I can work at my own pace, as long as I meet my deadlines. I can take a break for a few minutes, work in the evening if I have an appointment in the morning, or do whatever I need to. The routine is spiced up nicely by my travels for research—or for speaking engagements, which are happening more frequently now!

STATISTICS AND INFORMATION ABOUT THIS JOB

Authors like Natalie work under contract on each book, rather than drawing an annual salary. However, it is estimated that a full-time, professional writer can earn an average of $48,000 a year. The amount of money each contract is worth depends on several factors, including:

◆ The author's qualifications and expertise on the subject he or she is writing about; an established professional in the field can earn more money than a writer who must learn about the subject from scratch.

◆ The author's previous publishing experience; a writer with a proven track record can earn more money, especially if his or her earlier books sold well.

◆ The size and success of the publishing house; a large company with a big budget can offer more competitive contracts.

◆ The sales projections for the proposed book; something that is likely to be a best-seller is worth more than a specialized book that will only sell to a limited audience, and a very unique idea may be worth more than yet another book on a popular topic.

Authors can be paid in one of two ways: As a work-for-hire author, or as a royalty author with an advance. If the writing is a work-for-hire project, the author is paid a flat fee for the work (often with a first payment when the contract is signed, and the final payment upon completion of an acceptable manuscript). The author doesn't receive any additional money after the agreed-upon sum is paid, regardless of how well the book sells.

For royalty authors, the author is contracted to receive a percentage of the book's sales—called a *royalty.* The author also is typically paid an *advance* before the manuscript is complete to help pay expenses related to the writing of the book. These expenses may include office supplies, research costs, and book-related travel. Many authors use the services of agents, lawyers, and assistants, who get percentages of this money as well. This advance is actually like a loan against the royalty payments the author will receive. Once published, a book must sell a certain number of copies to "pay back" the advance amount, and after that, the author will begin receiving royalties on all copies sold.

Different publishing houses have different requirements for prospective authors. Some will only accept a completed manuscript if the author is new to them. Others have specific policies about how to submit pro-posals or manuscripts: in print or by e-mail; hand delivered or mailed; and, if printed, the number of pages and how it must be typed. It is best to check a publisher's Web site to be sure you are adhering to these poli-cies; otherwise, your submission may be automatically discarded.

Jennifer, a Rabbi
WHAT I DO

I am a Reform movement rabbi at a small suburban congregation. At this particular synagogue, I am the only paid employee. In my capacity as rabbi, I have many responsibilities. I teach, lead services, sing at the services, advise and counsel congregants, attend lots of meetings, par-ticipate in a lot of community and volunteer activities, sit on boards, make hospital visits, and conduct life-cycle rituals and activities. My teaching load this year includes three classes at my temple's religious school: the seventh grade class, where the kids are approaching bar- and bat-mitzvah age; the ninth grade class; and the tenth grade class. These last two classes are both preparing for confirmation, although they are separate. I also teach workshops and give lectures and other "one-shot" or short-term lessons, and I am occasionally called in to substitute or guest-speak at a nearby Jewish day school.

WHY I CHOSE THE EDUCATION MINOR

It's actually quite interesting. When my parents came up for Parents' Weekend during my first year of college, we were told that I was one of only three students in my year who had put down education as an interest! I come from a long line of teachers—most recently, my mother—so I grew up seeing teaching as a really worthwhile profession, and thanks to her example, I think I took to it right away. I wanted to have the skills involved in teaching, and I knew it would always be something I would have even if nothing else worked out.

When I first started college, I didn't initially plan to become a rabbi. But as soon as I knew that I wanted to be a rabbi, I knew that having an education background would be good preparation.

The college I went to didn't have an education major, since the university has a separate graduate school of education, but there *is* an education minor. As an undergrad, this worked out for me. I majored in religious studies, but was still able to take the education minor.

HOW THE EDUCATION MINOR PREPARED ME FOR MY JOB

In addition to classes, I ended up gaining experience in the classroom and writing curricula. One of my first rabbinic jobs was as assistant rabbi and director of education, and in that position, I ended up having to write a lot of the religious school curriculum and directing the teachers. My experiences in the education program also taught me to feel confident in front of a class full of students—and by extension, the congregation.

I learned a lot of helpful skills for teaching, such as managing the kids, planning lessons, and understanding special needs. It isn't enough to know a lot about a subject. A good teacher has to know how to convey what he or she knows to the students. I picked up a lot of good strategies from lectures, readings, and discussions in the program, and I got to try them out in my supervised student teaching. All the things I learned have helped me develop curriculum for my congregation's Hebrew school and work well with students, parents, and other teachers.

OTHER TRAINING

Even before college, I had gotten some experience working at a day care center. I also spent about five years teaching at a religious school, which gave me teaching assistant training and a chance to observe the strategies used by the more experienced teachers. Also, I had grown up participating in Jewish youth groups, and as I got older, I got to help lead activities for the younger children.

The student teaching and internship I did as part of the education minor were also important training experiences. During my junior year of college, I had an internship at a local public school, which involved teaching and observing once a week. Then, in my senior year, I had a student-teaching assignment three days a week at another public school. In addition to that, I also taught Hebrew school classes at a local temple near my college and continued to lead youth group activities and summer programs during vacation.

Another interesting internship I had in college was at Children's Television Workshop. As an intern, I was basically unpaid labor, but I did get to do some writing for one of their educational magazines for children. This also gave me more experience in applying my education skills to writing, which is certainly a good thing to know when I have to write sermons!

During college, I spent my junior year in Israel at Hebrew University. After graduation, I went into rabbinic school. I spent another year in Israel, this time as part of the rabbinic program, and when I came back to the States, I continued at a campus in a big city. But my student pulpits—the equivalent of student teaching for clergy—were in tiny communities, which really broadened my experience.

I also served in the United States Navy Chaplaincy Program during summer breaks, where I conducted services and taught and counseled members of the military.

Even after being ordained, I still try to keep up with new trends in education. In addition to the Reform Judaism conferences I go to as a rabbi, I regularly attend conventions and workshops of CAJE (The Conference for the Advancement of Jewish Education), which is just a terrific experience. I always come back with new ideas and materials, and I learn a lot from the lecturers and colleagues with whom I network.

HELPFUL MOVES

Getting into the classroom and applying what I was learning was the most helpful move for me. It was important for me to stretch the parameters and boundaries of education. Teaching should be both formal and informal, and there's a lot more room to expand the informal methods.

A practical bit of advice is to find good financial aid. Take out loans (and prepare to pay them back!), but also look for scholarships that you won't have to pay back. State governments and religious institutions have programs to help teachers-in-training. You just have to research which ones you qualify for.

I was told that a big reason a lot of colleges like mine don't have an education major is that we'd have to take a lot of the same courses in graduate school to get a master's degree and a permanent teaching license. But for me, it made sense to take the teaching courses while I was still in college. I wouldn't have been able to do that while I was in rabbinic school, and the skills I developed were just as useful in my student pulpits as they had been for student teaching.

Also, the variety of experiences I had in college and rabbinic school really prepared me for dealing with different kinds of people. As a rabbi, I never know who's going to walk into my office, and it's part of my job to immediately adjust my thinking to help whomever I'm dealing with at the moment.

PITFALLS TO AVOID

Be sure this is what you really want, because you're not going to make a million dollars doing it. The reward of a career like mine is in knowing what you're passing on to others and that you're improving their lives.

Whatever you do, don't burn any bridges! You never know who you're going to need help from for a letter of recommendation or an introduction to someone's cousin who's a realtor in the city where your new job is. Even on a personal level, you can't afford to alienate parents and congregants who might be able to recommend a good doctor or even a good blind date!

WHAT I LOVE ABOUT MY JOB

I love just about everything, except the politics (which I'll explain in a minute)!

I love meeting different kinds of people. I love teaching them about things that mean so much to me, being part of the special moments in their lives, or seeing that light bulb go on when they learn something new. I love seeing that shine in their eyes when they're inspired. I'm helping to improve the world as well as their lives.

THINGS ON THE JOB I COULD DO WITHOUT

There's a lot of politics in congregational life—I could really do without that! Everyone thinks what he or she has to say is more important than anyone else. My advice is to let the experts handle it. But sometimes there are people who like to throw their weight around, and I'm sometimes pressured to do special favors for someone who's donated a lot of money. It's hard to stand my ground when I know these same people will be deciding whether or not to renew my contract!

Sometimes it's hard to get personal time. I understand if people have an after-hours emergency, although no one likes to be woken up in the middle of the night by a phone call about bad news. What's difficult is having so few opportunities to go away for a weekend or holiday.

The Rabbinical Assembly of America recently released a report noting that after all these years, women rabbis still earn less money than their male colleagues. Many of us suspected as much, but it was still pretty shocking to have our suspicions confirmed. The rabbinic calling is a spiritual one, not one you'd pick to get rich. Still, I work hard, and it's insulting not to be fairly compensated.

MY WORK AND MY LIFE

Except for Saturdays and holidays, my mornings are not too stressful. I don't have to be at work quite as early as a schoolteacher, for example, so I can relax with my morning coffee and the paper and miss most of the rush hour traffic.

During a regular weekday, I spend time at my desk dealing with administrative business for the synagogue and all of its programs. This includes enrolling new members; ordering materials; fielding questions, problems, and requests from students, teachers, and parents; keeping track of the budget; and, of course, planning the curriculum. I also spend time writing sermons and newsletter columns. I plan services, especially the ones that need to be tailored for some special reason. I may have to adapt the same service for a youth group, for the elderly, or for a family celebration, so I try to make sure the music, sermon, and even refreshments are appropriate for each audience.

Sometimes my day includes various committee meetings concerning the Hebrew school or the temple as a whole. Some of those meetings, unfortunately, are in the evening to accommodate the committee members' schedules. I also take appointments in my office with potential new congregants, parents of the Hebrew school students, or people who are planning a life-cycle event, like a wedding.

There are times when I leave the office to pay hospital visits or make condolence calls. These are emotionally difficult, but the people are so grateful for the visit. I may also check out a site for an event, pick up supplies, or do other work-related business outside the office.

Being a rabbi is like being a doctor in some ways. I'm on 24/7! I never know when I'll have to be at the hospital until 10:00 p.m. I never know when something will come up and I'll have to cancel my personal plans. I've even gotten phone calls from congregants asking me to come bail them out of jail! My personal life has gone through a number of upheavals over the years. I've had to relocate several times as I moved from one job to the next.

Dating is hard, and I often think that no one who is single would want to be a rabbi if they knew what I know now. Even in the world of egalitarian Judaism, a lot of men are hesitant to date a rabbi, especially knowing that I'm in a career that may mean moving again the next time my contract expires. I also worry about the effect this kind of lifestyle could have on raising children—who may be pulled out of school and away from their friends every time Mommy gets a new job.

Still, there are great rewards to this job. I get to teach something that is so meaningful to me. As hard as this lifestyle has been for me, these kinds of intangible rewards make the job worthwhile.

STATISTICS AND INFORMATION ABOUT THIS JOB

Salaries for rabbis (and clergy of other religions) depend on a number of factors, such as the type of job (pulpit, teaching, hospital chaplain, and so on); type of community; type of hierarchy or administration; and type of experience the job candidate has.

Pulpit clergy like Jennifer are often given special bonuses such as *parsonage*, a sum of money beyond the salary that is meant to be used for housing expenses. Other congregations own a residence for their clergy to live in free of charge. These benefits are often part of the negotiation process.

For clergy specializing in education, as Jennifer does, salaries can range from $45,000 to $69,000. The median salary is about $56,000.

Dana, a Curriculum Designer
WHAT I DO

I create educational units on special topics to be taught in my community's elementary schools. The kind of special topics I deal with include things like personal safety, moral and ethical decision making, and tolerance. I often work with other specialists to design the curriculum for these topics; if it's a health issue, I might work with a school nurse, for instance. I also work with the regular classroom teachers to make sure the plans I make are well suited to the classes where they will be used. The lessons must be age-appropriate, for instance, and the activities must take into account the number of students in the room.

Because I'm still a licensed elementary school teacher, I also substitute in the classrooms when a teacher is out sick. I'm around anyway, so my presence can be handy if there's an emergency situation with a teacher.

WHY I CHOSE THE EDUCATION MAJOR

I've always loved working with kids, ever since I was old enough to start babysitting, so when I started college, I was glad to take a psychology course that involved observing children in school settings. As I watched the teachers in action, I felt that I could see myself doing what they were doing! That's when I really started to think about education as a major.

I wanted to learn more before I committed myself to the major, so I went to my campus career center. One of the things the advisor there did for me was to give me a career aptitude test, where I answered questions about my interests and preferences and the results suggest suitable careers. It came out that teaching was one of the careers on my list.

As a student, I may not have been at the top of my class, but I was (and still am) a hard worker. I think that's a good trait for a teacher to have, with all the preparation and details that need attention. It also sets a good example for the kids!

HOW THE EDUCATION MAJOR PREPARED ME FOR MY JOB

I took the coursework very seriously. Everything from the assigned readings to the classroom discussions to the student teaching and observation assignments were opportunities to learn about child development and learning theory, classroom management, and all the other issues in classroom teaching. Student teaching let me put what I was learning into practice.

Even though I'm not a regular classroom teacher anymore (although I do teach some of my special units myself), the things I learned in college are helpful for this job. I have a better understanding of the dynamics of a school, how kids learn at different ages, and, most importantly, how to write up a good lesson plan.

OTHER TRAINING

After college, I got my first teaching job and went to graduate school in the evening to get a master's degree and a permanent teaching license. My graduate school required a research thesis. I had become interested in the topic of moral education, which was getting some attention in the news at the time, so I decided to do my thesis on that. I used my own students to test the efficacy of a moral education unit, and found that a well-designed curriculum could positively affect the children's decision-making process (not that my kids were morally deficient in the first place!). This, in turn, got me interested in how teaching units of this sort could be used to help students learn about other important issues.

The assistant principal at the school where I was teaching had been very supportive about my graduate work and my research, and encouraged me to think about other ways these tactics could be used. She arranged for me to get some extra pay in return for working on similar projects that could be used in other classrooms. A couple of years later, a budget was approved that allowed me to be hired as a curriculum designer, and here I am!

Sometimes I attend seminars on the kinds of topics I design units for, like child abuse awareness or eating disorders. A lot of these conferences are during the day, and the district pays for me to go to them so I can stay up to date on the latest issues.

HELPFUL MOVES

I found it's important to take the time to understand what you're getting into and make the right decisions. That's what I did when I went to the career services office to learn more and took that aptitude test. Even observing experienced teachers at work was an example of this. Before I started college, I visited the campus and sat in on classes and talked to people to make sure I really wanted to go to that particular college, and I did the same thing when I started graduate school. Actually, I did something similar when I applied for my first teaching job. When I went for my interview, I took some extra time to visit classrooms (with permission, of course) and talk to teachers. I wanted to know if they were happy working at the school, if they felt the administration was supportive, how stressful the environment was, and things like that. When I got positive reactions to my questions and saw how good the school appeared, I looked forward to working there.

Also, seek out help and advice when you need it. Besides the career services advisor and the assistant principal I mentioned earlier, I also spent time with my college and grad school advisors. I went to professors for extra help when I felt I needed it. I even used the services of a dissertation coach when I was having trouble with some of the technical aspects of my thesis. I got to the coach through that nice assistant principal. The coach was very patient and good at explaining things, and she was worth the money I spent on her services. Some of my grad school classmates got help from typists, editors, translators (I had a lot of classmates whose first language was Spanish), and other people like that. I may not have needed those services, but they're other good examples of seeking help when you need it.

PITFALLS TO AVOID

I didn't run into too many problems, other than getting bogged down with too much work from time to time. One pitfall would be letting yourself fall too far behind in your work. For me, planning lessons, grading papers at work, and still having time to do my own homework while attending classes requires careful planning.

Another pitfall would be trying to do things without help. I almost made that mistake when I first started on my thesis because I had no way of knowing how hard it would be. Fortunately, I got help as soon as I realized I was in a little bit over my head!

WHAT I LOVE ABOUT MY JOB

I love the kids, of course. I have so much fun talking to them and hearing the ideas they come up with. As curriculum designer, I get to know more of the kids in the school than I would if I taught a single classroom, so it's even more fun for me now.

I also find this kind of curriculum planning very creative. Some parts of it are simply paperwork, and I've got that down to a science now. I enjoy thinking up activities to help the students learn, and I love designing materials, like posters and handouts, to be used in these lessons.

THINGS ON THE JOB I COULD DO WITHOUT

The downside to working with many classes is that I don't get to know one group of kids as intensely as I did before. I used to be much more aware of what was going on in my students' lives, like who had a new baby at home and whose grandmother was sick. Kids still talk to me about that stuff, especially if it relates to our special unit, but I may not see a particular child again for an update for quite a long time.

Another annoyance is the lack of time. There are so many things we want to cover in the course of the school year, and there never seems to be enough time. That makes it hard to squeeze in the units I design. Very often, we have to slot the units into the regular lessons. For instance, the moral education unit had stories to read, so I used part of the language arts time to read these stories.

The budget is another problem. I hate having to scale back my ideas because the school can't pay for the materials I want to use. Sometimes there are things like educational videos that I'd like to incorporate, but they are too expensive to use.

MY WORK AND MY LIFE

A really nice thing about my promotion to curriculum designer is that the lesson planning that I used to do after school hours is now part of my day job. Between that and finishing graduate school, I have my evenings free to spend with my boyfriend, who I think would have run out of patience if things hadn't improved! We're planning our future together, so it's good to have the time to meet with our parents and make all the arrangements we want. When we get married and have kids, I'll be especially glad to put work concerns behind me when I go home each day.

Public school hours are shorter than the usual business hours at a nine-to-five office, and because I don't have a regular classroom anymore, I rarely have to stay late. It's nice to have the rest of the afternoon to play in the city, whether I want to browse in a bookstore or run errands before the stores close. I just have to avoid the temptation to spend too much money!

Although my office hours are fairly regular, I do think about my job after work and on weekends, especially when I happen to see or hear something that gives me a new idea.

STATISTICS AND INFORMATION ABOUT THIS JOB

The median salary for curriculum developers in public schools in the United States is $57,000, with an approximate range of $46,000 to $68,000. Many school systems require a master's degree, although others will accept a bachelor's degree alone. Two to four years of experience in the field are also required.

Sarah, Assistant Principal and Program Coordinator
WHAT I DO

I am the assistant principal and program coordinator at a school-within-a-school, which is a special, self-contained school located within a larger school building, but independent of the larger school. My school is for gifted and talented children. Students must have a high enough IQ or other test scores to be admitted. In addition to administering the school, supervising teachers, and running interference with the Board of Education, I also am involved in the admissions process. Because the school has this special focus, I find myself acting as a sort of public relations liaison, coordinating visits from politicians and reporters and even showing VIPs around the building.

WHY I CHOSE THE EDUCATION MAJOR

I came to the United States as a child. I have a disabled sibling, so life wasn't always easy at home. School was an escape for me, as well as an opportunity to perfect my English and adjust to my new country. And like many immigrant children, I also became an unofficial teacher at an early age because I was the only one who could help my parents over the language and cultural barriers they faced. I think my parents were proud of my accomplishments in school, but there was still a lot of pressure on me to help the rest of the family.

I got married at a rather early age, which got me out of my parents' home, so I was already married when I went to a local public college. I gravitated toward the education major for several reasons. One, I already viewed school as a good place to be. Two, it was a career I could get into quickly and earn a living. Three, I knew that a teaching job would be compatible with family life, which was good, because I was already starting a family. Finally, with all the informal teaching I did at home, I think I just wanted to make sure I was doing it the right way!

How the Education Major Prepared Me for My Job

Public colleges tend to work closely with the state to comply with licensing requirements when it comes to education degrees. So in a very practical way, my major prepared me by getting me through whatever paperwork, required courses, and other regulations the state had at the time.

In a more day-to-day sense, the education major prepared me by honing my skills as a teacher, from communicating effectively to planning lessons to assessing students. I was pleased to find that I took to these things very easily.

Not only did these skills help me during my years as a classroom teacher, but they're just as important now as a principal. I still have to communicate well—to teachers, parents, and officials, as well as kids of all ages. I may not have to write all of the lesson plans myself, but I do have to know how to evaluate the ones my teachers submit. And the admissions process we use is just another type of student assessment.

Other Training

I very slowly earned a master's degree while I was teaching. It took me a long time because I was raising children of my own at the same time.

For a number of years after that, I continued to teach in a small religious school in my town. In return, my children were allowed to attend the school at a greatly discounted price. I loved the work, and I incorporated a lot of creative activities into my lessons. This was a great help when my husband was out of work for a while and money was tight!

After a few years, though, a new administration took over the school, and there was a real shift in the school population that made me very uncomfortable. The new administration had much different values than I do when it comes to education, particularly in terms of religion, and there was a lot of tension. I decided to leave the school as soon as I could, but I had to stay until my youngest child graduated, because we couldn't afford the tuition otherwise. It was really frustrating for a while! But it gave me time to decide what I wanted to do next, and to prepare for it.

Instead of just looking for a teaching job at another school, I decided to go back to graduate school and get a doctorate in education of the gifted. It was a field I had become interested in, in part because of the issues I was now dealing with at work. So for those last few semesters teaching at my children's school, I was also commuting to a nearby university and taking evening classes.

Helpful Moves

One of the most helpful resources I had was my family. My husband may not have my interest in higher education, and the kids couldn't understand why anyone would go back to school if she didn't have to, but they respected my goals, and they did a lot to help make it possible for me to return to school while still teaching and running a house. My husband really pitched in around the house, chauffeuring the kids around when I had to go to evening classes, and picking me up from the station when I got home late. He and my children did what they could to help out so there would be less housework for me to do. Even though my schedule was hard on them (and on me!), they tried to encourage me and be as supportive as they could be.

Pitfalls to Avoid

Part of me wants to say, "don't lose your appointment book," but looking back at all the unexpected things that got penciled into mine, I think it's more important to not be rigid. Yes, you want to be disciplined and have your hours for school, for work, and for family, but you also have to be realistic. Stuff happens, and you have to be flexible enough to adapt.

What I Love About My Job

I'm happy with the way we've made the program work for our kids. The school is a comfortable, homey environment where the kids can relax and enjoy learning. Some of these kids are so bright that they really don't fit in at other kinds of schools, so it's good to see them thriving here.

Things on the Job I Could Do Without

Bureaucracy has always been a problem in schools, but for a specialized school like mine, it's an even bigger problem. The district is always instituting new methods of teaching, which often means switching from one model to the next each year, and that's really inconsistent for students and teachers alike. And these orders come from people in offices somewhere who don't spend the day in the classroom and don't have the same kind of first-hand knowledge of what works and what needs to be changed. On top of that, these district-wide orders are given with the district's average school setting in mind, but they're imposed across the board, even at a special program like mine that is a completely different kind of setting. Recently, I had a confrontation over the type of testing that was being used in my school. I was told that it was now considered unsuitable for the average pupil in this district. But my students are not average pupils, and the alternatives being offered just won't work here!

I could also do without the money problems. Special programs are always the first ones to be cut, and I'm forced to do more with less. I also find that I'm putting in more and more hours for the same pay, because I can't hire someone else to help me.

My Work and My Life

I put in very long hours now, and that's only partially because of my long commute. As I mentioned, I've essentially been doing the work of two people, so it takes a long time. I wouldn't have been able to do this when my kids were little and needed me around a lot, so it's a good thing this is a second career for me.

Some day, I would like to start my own program for gifted children and do things the way I want to. Doing things this way is incredibly frustrating for me and for the other people involved. But I still believe in education of the gifted.

STATISTICS AND INFORMATION ABOUT THIS JOB

The median salary for public school assistant principals in the United States is $56,000, with an approximate range of $48,000 to $62,000. Assistant principals who work in specialized schools like Sarah's, and who often have additional training and experience for that specialty, can draw salaries closer to the top of the range. Most school systems require a graduate degree and several years of experience in the field.

Vicky, Tutoring Center Co-Owner
WHAT I DO

I am a partner at a private academic tutoring center that specializes in helping otherwise bright students with learning disabilities get through school and apply successfully to competitive colleges. As the partner with the education degree, my responsibilities include assessing students and planning a course of action that will best help them.

Right after graduating from college, I taught full time in a local public school. After that, I went to work for a large, well-known test-preparation company and stayed there for a couple of years. After a while, a former coworker who started the center where I now work recruited me to teach for her. The business became successful, and when it was time to expand, she took me on as a partner. So while her responsibilities lie in the business end of things, I'm the partner with the teaching expertise.

WHY I CHOSE THE EDUCATION MAJOR

I think I was much more idealistic than realistic when I started college. Among my peers at the time, teaching had come back into vogue as a way to change the world, almost like a holy calling. It sounded like a good plan: working with children who would love me, of course, raising them up through education, and refusing to "sell out" by going to work for some mega-corporation. So I signed up for the education major and took a lot of classes that reinforced ideas like that. There was a lot of discussion about how education could rescue children from at-risk homes and improve society. It sounded like a modern-day answer to the concept of missionaries.

How the Education Major Prepared Me for My Job

Although I don't work in a school, so much of the training I had as an education major applies to my job. I evaluate students' needs and progress, just as a schoolteacher would. I prepare lessons and talk to parents, just like a schoolteacher. I even help students with college applications, just as I remember my high school teachers doing with me!

Other Training

My original plan was to spend a year or two teaching full time, and then go back to graduate school part time for the required master's degree. But by the end of my first year teaching in public school, I realized that this was not for me. Reality was setting in. The kids who I thought would love me were disrespectful, the parents were indifferent, the administration was unsupportive, and the pay was not enough to cover my college loans. The school was in a bad neighborhood and I didn't feel safe going to work. My idealism had bumped up against reality, and I just wanted to get out of that school. But now that I was falling behind with those loans, I had to think hard about what to do instead that could use the training I already had.

I had already started looking into teaching an SAT course for one of the big preparation companies, which I could do part time to supplement my teaching income. I went through a training program for one of the companies, and I did well enough that when another tutor got sick, I was asked to take on his class as well. The company also offers private tutoring, and I was able to do some of that, especially for one of the foreign-language SAT II tests. (There aren't enough students taking it to form a class, so those kids get tutored instead.) The company paid well, and I realized that if I could get enough students and classes, I could quit teaching at the public school! It wasn't a permanent solution, but it would tide me over until I could figure out what to do "for real."

I found that I liked this work. Although the environment was more informal than the school (the kids called us by our first names, for example), the students were serious about their future and related to me much better than the kids at the public school did. They and their parents valued my judgment and appreciated my feedback. The company provided all the necessary materials and was available to help me when I needed it. The training and the actual experience of teaching really helped me develop a lot of the skills I use now.

One woman had helped train me to teach the SAT course, and she was like a mentor to me. We became good friends and stayed in touch even after she left the company. She and a college buddy of hers had come up with an idea for a tutoring business and it was becoming successful. As the business grew, it began offering more services and taking on more clients, which meant having to hire more people. So my friend called me up and asked me to come work for her.

At first, I tutored high school students in their regular academic subjects. Under the terms of my contract with the big test-prep company, I wasn't allowed to teach another SAT course for a year, but when the year was up, I began to do that again, too. When my friend expanded the company again, she asked me to become the partner in charge of the tutoring division. The other partner was in charge of the college guidance division, and my friend handles the business matters.

Helpful Moves

I'm glad I took advantage of the opportunities that came my way. When that coworker got sick, I took on the extra class so I could make more money. When my mentor/friend offered me a job and then a partnership, I took on those challenges as well. I certainly didn't rush into these things—I'm much more leery of acting too quickly since the whole public school experience! I took the time to ask questions and consider the pros and cons. I've learned a lot about making informed decisions!

To help make some of these decisions, I consulted a financial counselor at my bank. I wanted to be sure I wasn't getting myself into a worse situation by leaving the big test-prep company, for example. The counselor sat down with me and went over all the relevant data and really helped me understand the risks and benefits. The counselor also let me know about some special programs offered by the bank to help me make this transition.

On another financial front, I was the third partner to join the business, so by the time I got there, the other two women had already gotten the business off the ground. For me, this meant that I didn't have to take on the monetary risk of starting a new company, and I didn't have to invest my own money in it.

PITFALLS TO AVOID

My personal pitfall was the opposite of making an informed decision. It's clear to me now that I went into the education major and the public school job with the proverbial rose-colored glasses on. In my idealism, I failed to consider the hardships I would face and the realities of the people I'd be working with. Having ideals is a good thing, but I just didn't take the time to look at the downside. When my first job didn't turn out the way I'd imagined it, I was really shocked! I learned the hard way to research a situation before I make a decision.

I almost had another pitfall as the new partner. Initially, I felt like the junior partner and was a little uncomfortable suggesting changes to the people whose dream this was originally. But I soon realized that my partners were open to my suggestions. The one who had been my mentor assured me that they wanted to hear my ideas, and that was one of the reasons they invited me to join the business. She made our meetings so positive and relaxed that I got over my fears after a while, and now I feel like an equal partner.

WHAT I LOVE ABOUT MY JOB

One of my favorite things on the job is the success stories. A student comes to me struggling with a subject in school or on a test, and after we work together, we can see the improvement in the student's scores. I didn't often get that feeling as a schoolteacher.

I also like the way we all work together. The parents, students, and I all have the same goal in mind, even if the kid would rather be hanging out with friends. They view me as an expert and as someone who's here to help. I like the feeling of being respected for my professional knowledge and using it in a non-adversarial situation.

THINGS ON THE JOB I COULD DO WITHOUT

There isn't much that I don't like on this job. My old idealistic streak flares up once in a while to remind me that I'm working with well-off suburban kids now, instead of needy inner-city children, but let's face it, I wasn't succeeding with the inner-city children. The things that bother me are relatively small annoyances, such as when the SATs were revamped a few years ago and we had to adapt to that. And because some of my students have dyslexia and similar learning disabilities, sometimes there are silly mix-ups over scheduling or even filling out the answer forms!

MY WORK AND MY LIFE

Because our clients are in school during the day, the heavy part of my schedule comes later in the day. Fortunately, the kids have to be back at school the next morning, so although I work later than I did as a schoolteacher, it's not excessive.

During the earlier part of the day, I deal with administrative issues, such as reviewing job applicants, keeping up with curricula and tests, and matching students up with the right tutors. I also take phone calls from parents and teachers. A couple of times a week, my two partners and I have lunch together so we can discuss business matters and keep each other up to date on our respective areas of the company. The three of us get along very well, so even working lunches like these can be a lot of fun!

When I gave up my school job, the biggest sacrifice for me was the loss of medical insurance. As difficult as that job was, and as bad as the pay was, the benefits were pretty good. My next job didn't offer benefits to the tutors, since most of us were part-timers. The package my current partners offered was a big incentive for me to go to work with them!

As one of the partners in the company, I have a lot more freedom about arranging vacations and taking personal time. We agreed that as long as none of us abuse the privilege, we could be more flexible about things like that. We just make sure to keep one another aware of our schedules. After the bureaucracy I dealt with in the past, I find this very refreshing!

STATISTICS AND INFORMATION ABOUT THIS JOB

Because Vicky is an entrepreneur and member of a business partnership, her earnings are at the level of an educational consultant, rather than a tutor who gets paid by the hour. The median annual income for this type of work exceeds $80,000.

Josh, a Museum Educator
WHAT I DO

I design educational exhibits for children at a small- to mid-sized museum. I also lead workshops and activities for kids and their families.

The exhibits I design are often hands-on. Kids—and sometimes adults—can't resist touching things, which was always a no-no at traditional museum exhibits, so part of my job is to make sure there are a lot of things to touch and manipulate in the exhibits I design. It might be a panel with swatches of materials similar to the ones used in some priceless art, so the kids can find out what the stuff feels like, or it might be controls the kids can manipulate, like colorful buttons to start a recording. I also have to make sure that the little signs explaining things are written in words kids can understand.

The workshops are a lot of fun. Sometimes I'm really just teaching, especially when large groups of kids come to the museum on a class trip. Then my job is to tell them about the exhibits they're seeing in a way that they'll understand and enjoy. A lot of kids think museums are boring, so I try to show them that museums can be fun, even if I have to joke around with them. Other times, I'm leading an activity with the kids. It could be an art project, where the kids get to try out the techniques used by the artists of the works on display, or a "let's pretend" session, where they act out the roles in a historical or cultural event. Around holidays, I even bring my guitar to work and lead sing-alongs, teaching songs from other cultures and reintroducing old favorites.

Museums often produce books based on current exhibits, and I get to work on some of those, too.

WHY I CHOSE THE EDUCATION MAJOR

I grew up in a great community where families were very active and there were a lot of great programs for kids. Some of the older kids and grownups I looked up to the most were the ones who would lead these programs. They were just so funny and positive, and they seemed to be doing fun stuff all day (at least when I saw them), instead of wearing a suit and tie in a boring office. Eventually, I became one of the older kids and helped run programs for the younger ones, and I had such a great time playing games and things like that. Maybe I just didn't want to give up that part of being a kid! So I started to think about careers that would let me keep doing that sort of thing. I wasn't sure if I wanted to be a regular teacher—too much marking tests and homework—but I thought I might find an interesting specialty. Then I learned that some of the adults I had been looking up to actually had degrees in community service and did this full time for a living, which I thought was very cool. I thought I'd enjoy working at a Y or some other kind of community center. It would be like summer camp year-round!

I went to a good state college not far from where I grew up, and I started off with the education courses. But the school wanted education majors to take a second major as well, so I also majored in sociology, which I became interested in after taking the introductory course for my social sciences requirement.

HOW THE EDUCATION MAJOR PREPARED ME FOR MY JOB

As a museum educator, it's important for me to know how to design exhibits and activities that help visitors learn about whatever is on display, and learning to develop lesson plans for regular classroom teaching was good practice. I learned to clearly state the goal of the lesson (or in my case, the exhibit or activity) and take the right steps to get there.

I also found the course work that covered the needs of children at different ages very helpful. Because I'm not teaching one class and one grade level, I have to be ready for kids of all ages to come through the museum, so it's a good thing I know how to talk to them all!

I should also mention how my other major helped. I didn't know at the time that I'd end up working in a museum, but my sociology background turned out to be very helpful. Obviously, a lot of people who work in museums have backgrounds in things like art history, like some of my coworkers, but since I deal with music and ethnic history as well as with art, sociology was good preparation for me.

OTHER TRAINING

I thought I'd end up working at a community center, but a friend of a friend recommended me for the museum job. At the time, the museum was making a big push to add more child-friendly exhibits, and the director of education wanted to hire someone who was creative and who also had the right kind of personality—childish, I guess!—to relate to kids.

The museum, which is affiliated with a local university, offers its employees reduced tuition as part of their benefits. So after working there for a few years, I took advantage of this benefit and went back for a master's degree in museum education, which was the kind of program you design yourself in conjunction with the school. It meant taking classes in departments as far-flung as architecture (for designing exhibits) to child psychology to ethnic studies. It was hard work getting the degree while working at the museum, but it was really interesting.

A lot of my informal experience was good training, too. Everything from being a summer camp counselor to a youth group leader helped me learn to relate better to the kids and manage them in a group setting. Acting in high school and college plays was good training for speaking in public (loudly, clearly, and entertainingly!), especially because museum presentations, like lesson plans, follow a kind of script. Even working with other counselors and leaders trained me to work well with a planning committee—namely my boss and the other three people in the department—and to see a group project through until the end.

Helpful Moves

The best thing I can say is to do something you enjoy. And be creative enough to consider how you can make a career out of some hobby or favorite activity. I didn't know much about museum education as a career, but when my friend's friend met me and said she thought I'd be perfect for the job, I didn't dismiss what she said just because I had planned to work at a community center; I'm glad I gave it some consideration.

I also recommend taking advantage of opportunities to advance yourself at work. I might not have thought about going to graduate school when I did if my supervisor hadn't suggested that I take some classes at the university with my employee discount. Getting that degree resulted in a salary increase and more responsibilities at work, and I think I was ready for both of those things by the time I did them!

Pitfalls to Avoid

I think that if I'd known I would end up working at a museum, I might have taken more art history and related courses in college.

This job requires a lot of energy and creativity, so if those aren't your strong points, you might want to reconsider the job. You can't appear listless and tired in front of a group of six-year-old museum goers, and you can't make a half-hearted effort at creating a new exhibit that turns out to be the same old thing.

One thing this job does not offer is a huge amount of money. Museums aren't the wealthiest institutions around, and most of the money goes into acquiring and maintaining the things that are on exhibit. Even with my new degree, I'm not the leading authority in the field, and even with the accompanying pay raise, I'm not going to make the *Forbes* list! So don't make the mistake of expecting to get rich working at a museum.

What I Love About My Job

I love that I get to do fun stuff all day, just like I imagined when I was a kid. I love getting to play and experiment with materials, and I love doing creative activities for a living. I don't even have to dress up for work, because I often have to sit on the floor with a circle of kids and do messy activities.

I don't know if it's my level of creativity or just a short attention span, but I really enjoy having a variety of different things to do in the course of the day. I spend time with museum visitors, but I also get to work behind the scenes, and in different rooms with different kinds of exhibits. Too much sameness would get to me at a more conventional job!

I like seeing all the different people who come into the museum. They're all ages, and from all backgrounds, and some of them—especially the really little ones—ask the funniest questions! Sometimes I think they entertain me more than I entertain them.

It also feels great to walk around the museum and see all the different things that I had a hand in putting together. Even if I'm just walking through a gallery on my way back to my office, I might hear some kid going, "Mommy, Mommy, look at this neat thing!"

One thing I really love about my job is the perks. In addition to benefits like the tuition break, I also get to travel to see museum exhibits in other cities or even other countries. And the people I work with make my job a really great place to be. There's a sort of family feeling—we look out for each other and for the museum.

THINGS ON THE JOB I COULD DO WITHOUT

Some days are just really bad at work. There are days when it rains and people track in mud and the floor gets slippery and someone falls down, and then a kid wanders away from his group and no one can find him, and another kid gets scared and starts crying, and I've had to deal with all of it. I've even had kids throw up on my shoes. But as a museum employee, I have to keep a pleasant face and assure everyone that "it's no trouble at all."

Then there are policy issues. As a museum, we're very dependent on donations, of course, but sometimes a big donor will make some kind of special request that makes my work harder. For example, someone might donate or loan a particular work of art for an exhibit, and insist that it be displayed in the center of the gallery, even though it doesn't make sense historically to put it there, or the lighting is wrong. In those situations, we have to find a way to make the request work or else we won't be allowed to use the piece in question, and the donor might get insulted and not want to help us anymore. Along the same lines, it drives me crazy when I work for days on end to develop an exhibit for young children, and then a wealthy board member tells us we have to take it down because his grandchild said it was "too hard."

Money can also be an issue—not in terms of my salary, but in terms of how it affects my work. When we plan a workshop or exhibit, we have to keep the budget in mind. And because we're dealing with underage kids as well as with valuable art and artifacts, there are additional expenditures we have to factor in, like insurance or childproof safety devices. We may not be able to use a building material we want because it's not approved for use around children, so we have to use something else that's more expensive, which may then mean we can't afford as much of it, so the whole exhibit has to be scaled down. At times like that, it's a good thing I'm the grown-up now and can handle the disappointment!

MY WORK AND MY LIFE

I work under the head of the museum education department, who is the most senior member of our team and has much more advanced training and experience. I have two full-time coworkers, one of whom is around my age, and the other who is a few years younger and is the junior member. There are also a handful of part-timers and volunteers who change every so often, so the numbers aren't always the same. They include high school kids who work here to fulfill a community service requirement, interns preparing for their own careers, and docents, who lead tours of many of the exhibits I help design.

The museum doesn't open as early as most workplaces, but staffers like me come in early. I more or less keep normal business hours, although sometimes I stay late for an evening event I'm involved with, or to make a presentation to the board of trustees, who meet after work, as many of them have jobs elsewhere. Generally, though, I do have time for a nice social life and to do other things I like on my own time.

My typical day at work includes meetings about upcoming or ongoing projects, planning an exhibit or activity in the office and then setting it up in one of the gallery rooms, and leading a workshop or two. Some of the workshops are planned for a specific group, like an activity scheduled for the fourth grade class that's coming in after lunch, while others are part of the routine schedule, especially on weekend and other non-school days, when lots of kids come in with their parents. Before each workshop, I have to make sure I have enough materials and do any other preparation that's needed.

Less often, I have to stay late for those after-hours meetings and events, like an opening and reception for a new exhibit. I don't always have to be the one to do that, but sometimes I have to at least help, even if it isn't an exhibit I worked on. At least these things are scheduled in advance. I know people like lawyers who are always having last-minute emergencies, canceling meetings and staying at the office until late in the evening. I'm really glad I don't have to do that!

A few times a year, the museum sends me out of town to meet with the people at other museums, to get ideas, or to report back on an exhibit that's received a lot of good press. These trips are planned well in advance, so it's not disruptive to my personal life, and some of them are actually in the same city as my museum, so I don't have to go far. When I do go out of town, I may have time to see more of the city I'm visiting, or even get together with friends who live close by, so I usually enjoy these trips, especially since I don't have to pay for them!

STATISTICS AND INFORMATION ABOUT THIS JOB

The median salary for museum educators in the United States is $34,000, with an approximate range of $31,000 to $39,000, although it can be higher in major cities. Most employers require several years of experience in a related field. An advanced degree is a plus, but it isn't necessary unless you're hoping to land a senior position. Some states do offer a license in the field, but you can usually earn it as you work under the supervision of a more experienced educator.

Resources

Selecting a career is one of the most important decisions of your life. The more information you have, the better you'll feel about whether the decision you made was the right one. This appendix is a handy reference to other resources you can explore before committing yourself to a career in education.

Education Organizations

American Association for Higher Education (AAHE)
http://aahe.org
One Dupont Circle, Ste. 360
Washington, DC 20036
Phone: 202-293-6440 / Fax: 202-293-0073

American Association of Christian Schools (AACS)
http://aacs.org
2000 Vance Ave.
Chattanooga, TN 37404
Phone: 423-629-4280 / Fax: 423-622-7461

**American Association of Colleges for
Teacher Education (AACTE)**
http://aacte.org
1307 New York Ave. NW, Suite 300
Washington, DC 20005-4701
Phone: 202-293-2450 / Fax: 202-457-8095

American Association of Physics Teachers (AAPT)
http://aapt.org
One Physics Ellipse
College Park, MD 20740-3845
Phone: 301-209-3311

**American Association of State Colleges
and Universities (AASCU)**
http://aascu.org
1307 New York Ave. NW, Fifth Floor
Washington, DC 20005-1701
Phone: 202-293-7070 / Fax: 202-296-5819

**American Association of Teachers of Spanish
and Portuguese (AATSP)**
http://aatsp.org
423 Exton Commons
Exton, PA 19341-2451
Phone: 610-363-7005 / Fax: 610-363-7116

American Council on Education (ACE)
http://acenet.edu
One Dupont Circle NW
Washington, DC 20036
Phone: 202-939-9300

**American Council on the Teaching
of Foreign Languages (ACTFL)**
http://actfl.org
700 S. Washington St., Ste. 210
Alexandria, VA 22314
Phone: 703-894-2900 / Fax: 703-894-2905

American Counseling Association
http://www.counseling.org
5999 Stevenson Ave.
Alexandria, VA 22304
Phone: 800-347-6647 / Fax: 800-473-2329

American Federation of Teachers (AFT)
http://aft.org
555 New Jersey Ave. NW
Washington, DC 20001

Carnegie Foundation for the Advancement of Teaching
http://carnegiefoundation.org/index.htm
51 Vista Lane
Stanford, CA 94305
Phone: 650-566-5100

Council for American Private Education (CAPE)
http://capenet.org
13017 Wisteria Dr. #457
Germantown, MD 20874
Phone: 301-916-8460 / Fax: 301-916-8485

Council for Higher Education Accreditation (CHEA)
http://chea.org
One Dupont Circle NW, Ste. 510
Washington, DC 20036
Phone: 202-955-6126 / Fax: 202-955-6129

Kappa Delta Pi (PDI)
http://www.kdp.org
3707 Woodview Trace
Indianapolis, IN 46268-1158
Phone: 800-284-3167 / 317-704-2323

National Art Education Association (NAEA)
http://naea-reston.org
1916 Association Dr.
Reston, VA 20191-1590
Phone: 703-860-8000 / Fax: 703-860-2960

**National Association for the Education
of Young Children (NAEYC)**
http://naeyc.org
1509 16th St. NW
Washington, DC 20036
Phone: 202-232-8777

National Association of Biology Teachers (NABT)
http://nabt.org
12030 Sunrise Valley Dr., Ste. 110
Reston, VA 20191
Phone: 703-264-9696 or 800-406-0775 / Fax: 703-264-7778

National Business Education Association (NBEA)
http://nbea.org
1914 Association Dr.
Reston, VA 20191-1596
Phone: 703-860-8300 / Fax: 703-620-4483

National Catholic Educational Association (NCEA)
http://ncea.org
1077 30th St. NW, Ste. 100
Washington, DC 20007-3852
Phone: 202-337-6232 / Fax: 202-333-6706

**National Council for Accreditation
of Teacher Education (NCATE)**
http://ncate.org
2010 Massachusetts Ave. NW, Ste. 500
Washington, DC 20036-1023
Phone: 202-466-7496 / Fax: 202-296-6620

National Council for Geographic Education (NCGE)
http://ncge.org
Jacksonville State University
206A Martin Hall
Jacksonville, AL 36265-1602
Phone: 256-782-5293 / Fax: 256-782-5336

National Council for History Education (NCHE)
http://www.history.org/nche
26915 Westwood Rd., Ste. B-2
Westlake, OH 44145
Phone: 440-835-1776 / Fax: 440-835-1295

National Council for the Social Studies (NCSS)
http://ncss.org
8555 Sixteenth St.
Silver Spring, MD 20910

National Council for Teachers of English (NCTE)
http://www.ncte.org
1111 W. Kenyon Rd.
Urbana, IL 61801-1096
Phone: 217-328-3870 or 877-369-6283

National Council of Teachers of Mathematics (NCTM)
http://nctm.org
1906 Association Dr.
Reston, VA 20191-1502
Phone: 703-620-9840 / Fax: 703-476-2970

National Education Association (NEA)
http://nea.org
1201 16th St., NW
Washington, DC 20036-3290
Phone: 202-833-4000

Teacher Education Accreditation Council (TEAC)
http://teac.org
One Dupont Circle, Ste. 320
Washington, DC 20036-0110
Phone: 202-466-7236 / Fax: 202-466-7238

United States Department of Education (USDOE)
http://ed.gov/Programs/EROD
400 Maryland Ave. SW
Washington, DC 20202-0498

Books and Magazines
BOOKS

Careers in Education, VGM Career Books, New York, 2004.
Contains a complete listing of educational organizations, and such additional information on education careers as salaries, retirement packages, and benefits.

College Majors Handbook, JIST Works, Indianapolis, IN, 2004.
While the chapter on education majors is only one of 60, this book does offer insight into the future outlook for education careers, as well as salary ranges, and an overview of what job candidates can expect on the job.

Graduate Programs in Education 2004, Thomson Learning/Peterson's Publishing, Lawrenceville, NJ, 2003.
At more than 1,600 pages, this tome includes all U.S. colleges that offer graduate programs in education, as well as their contact information.

U.S. News & World Report Ultimate Guide to Becoming a Teacher, Sourcebooks, Inc., Naperville, IL, 2004.
Not only does the magazine offer annual college rankings in such programs as education, it also publishes this guide to current topics affecting the field of education and detailed rankings on such topics as the "smallest" and "largest" schools of education in the United States. The book also offers a state-by-state listing of universities offering graduate degrees in education.

MAGAZINES

Academic Exchange Quarterly
http://www.rapidintellect.com/AEQweb/

Current Issues in Education
http://cie.asu.edu/

Education Next: A Journal of Opinions Research
http://www.educationnext.org/

Education Review
http://edrev.asu.edu/index.html

Education Today
http://www.education-today.co.nz/

Education Week
http://www.edweek.org/

Horizon
http://horizon.unc.edu/

International Journal of Education & the Arts
http://ijea.asu.com.

Journal of Educational Media and Hypermedia (JEMH)
http://www.aace.org/pubs/jemh/default.htm.

The Journal of Higher Education (JHE)
http://www.ohiostatepress.org/Journals/JHE/jhemain.htm.

The Journal of Research in Childhood Education (JRCE)
http://www..udel.edu/bateman/acei/jrcehp.htm.

The Journal of Research on Technology in Education
http://www. iste.org/jrte/37/1/index.cfm.

The Journal of Special Education
http://www.proedinc/jse.html.

Learners Online
http://www.learnersonline.com/

Liberal Education
http://aacu-edu.org/liberaleducation/index.cfm.

Media and Methods Magazine Online
http://www.media-methods.com/

MultiCultural Review
http://www.mcreview.com/

NEA Today
http://www.nea.org/neatoday/0411

Rethinking Schools Online
http://www.rethinkingschools.org/

The School Administrator
http://www.aasa.org/publications/sa/index.htm.

TCRecord.org: The Voice of Scholarship in Education
http://www.tcrecord.org/

Teacher Librarian: The Journal for School Library Professionals
http://www.teacherlibrarian.com/

Teaching K-8 Magazine: Teacher Resources for Professional Development
http://www.teachingk-8.com/

The Times Higher Education Supplement
http://www.thes.co.uk/

Index

A

NOTES

Notes

NOTES

NOTES

NOTES